W9-AVX-235

NEW BRIGHTON HIGH SCHOOL
NEW BRIGHTON, PA 15066

NEW BRIGHTON HIGH SCHOOL

13597   345.73 K00
Leopold and Loeb : teen

Leopold and Loeb
Teen Killers

by Andy Koopmans

San Diego • Detroit • New York • San Francisco • Cleveland
New Haven, Conn. • Waterville, Maine • London • Munich

NEW BRIGHTON HIGH SCHOOL
NEW BRIGHTON, PA 15066

Other books in the Famous Trials series:

© 2004 by Lucent Books. Lucent Books is an imprint of The Gale Group, Inc.,
a division of Thomson Learning, Inc.

Lucent Books® and Thomson Learning™ are trademarks used herein under license.

For more information, contact
Lucent Books
27500 Drake Rd.
Farmington Hills, MI 48331-3535
Or you can visit our Internet site at http://www.gale.com

ALL RIGHTS RESERVED.
No part of this work covered by the copyright hereon may be reproduced or used in any form or by any means—graphic, electronic, or mechanical, including photocopying, recording, taping, Web distribution, or information storage retrieval systems—without the written permission of the publisher.

LIBRARY OF CONGRESS CATALOGING-IN-PUBLICATION DATA

Koopmans, Andy.
   Leoplold and Loeb: teen killers / by Andy Koopmans.
      v. cm. — (Famous trials)
Includes bibliographical references and index.
Summary: Discusses the notorious trial of teenagers Nathan Leopold Jr. and Richard Loeb, who, on May 21, 1924, abducted and murdered a fourteen-year-old boy. Includes discussion of the backgrounds of the two young murderers and their victim, the psychological ramifications of the crime, and famed civil rights attorney Clarence Darrow's defense strategy.
Contents: Kidnapping in Kenwood — Manhunt — A perfect crime — An airtight case — Men of diseased minds — Showdown and decision.
      ISBN 1-59018-227-8 (Hardback : alk. paper)
      1. Loeb, Richard A., 1905 or 6-1936 — Trials, litigation, etc. — Juvenile literature. 2. Leopold, Nathan Freudenthal, 1904 or 5-1971 — Trials, litigation, etc. — Juvenile litera-ture. 3. Trials (Murder) — Illinois — Cook County — Juvenile literature. 4. Trials (Kid-napping) — Illinois — Cook County — Juvenile literature. [1. Loeb, Richard A., 1905 or 6-1936 — Trials, litigation, etc. 2. Leopold, Nathan Freudenthal, 1904 or 5-1971— Trials, litigation, etc. 3. Trials (Murder) 4. Trials (Kidnapping) 5. Murder.] I. Title. II. Series.
      KF224.L46K66 2004
      345.73'02523 — dc22

                                                                    2003015070

Printed in the United States of America

Table of Contents

Foreword

"The law is not an end in and of itself, nor does it provide ends. It is preeminently a means to serve what we think is right."

William J. Brennan Jr.

THE CONCEPT OF JUSTICE AND THE RULE OF LAW are hallmarks of Western civilization, manifested perhaps most visibly in widely famous and dramatic court trials. These trials include such important and memorable personages as the ancient Greek philosopher Socrates, who was accused and convicted of corrupting the minds of his society's youth in 399 B.C.; the French maiden and military leader Joan of Arc, accused and convicted of heresy against the church in 1431; to former football star O.J. Simpson, acquitted of double murder in 1995. These and other well-known and controversial trials constitute the most public, and therefore most familiar, demonstrations of a Western legal tradition that dates back through the ages. Although no one is certain when the first law code appeared or when the first formal court trials were held, Babylonian ruler Hammurabi introduced the first known law code in about 1760 B.C. It remains unclear how this code was administered, and no records of specific trials have survived. What is clear, however, is that humans have always sought to govern behavior and define actions in terms of law.

Almost all societies have made laws and prosecuted people for going against those laws, but the question of which behaviors to sanction and which to censure has always been controversial and remains in flux. Some, such as Roman orator and legislator Cicero, argue that laws are simply applications of universal standards. Cicero believed that humanity would agree on what constituted illegal behavior and that human laws were a mere extension of natural laws. "True law is right reason in agreement with nature," he wrote, world-wide in scope, unchanging, everlasting. . . .We may not oppose or alter that law, we cannot abolish it, we cannot be freed from its obligations by any legislature. . . .This [natural] law does not differ for Rome and for Athens, for the present and for the future. . . . It is and will be valid for all nations and all times.

Cicero's rather optimistic view has been contradicted throughout history, however. For every law made to preserve harmony and set universal standards of behavior, another has been born of fear, prejudice, greed, desire for power, and a host of other motives. History is replete with individuals defying and fighting to change such laws—and even to topple governments that dictate such laws. Abolitionists fought against slavery, civil rights leaders fought for equal rights, millions throughout the world have fought for independence—these constitute a minimum of reasons for which people have sought to overturn laws that they believed to be wrong or unjust. In opposition to Cicero, then, many others, such as eighteenth-century English poet and philosopher William Godwin, believe humans must be constantly vigilant against bad laws. As Godwin said in 1793:

> Laws we sometimes call the wisdom of our ancestors. But this is a strange imposition. It was as frequently the dictate of their passion, of timidity, jealousy, a monopolizing spirit, and a lust of power that knew no bounds. Are we not obliged perpetually to renew and remodel this misnamed wisdom of our ancestors? To correct it by a detection of their ignorance, and a censure of their intolerance?

Lucent Books' *Famous Trials* series showcases trials that exemplify both society's praiseworthy condemnation of universally unacceptable behavior, and its misguided persecution of individuals based on fear and ignorance, as well as trials that leave open the question of whether justice has been done. Each volume begins by setting the scene and providing a historical context to show how society's mores influence the trial process and the verdict.

Each book goes on to present a detailed and lively account of the trial, including liberal use of primary source material such as direct testimony, lawyers' summations, and contemporary and modern commentary. In addition, sidebars throughout the text create a broader context by presenting illuminating details about important points of law, information on key personalities, and important distinctions related to civil, federal, and criminal procedures. Thus, all of the primary and secondary source material included in both the text and the sidebars demonstrates to readers the sources and methods historians use to derive information and conclusions about such events.

Lastly, each *Famous Trials* volume includes one or more of the following comprehensive tools that motivate readers to pursue further reading and research. A timeline allows readers to see the scope of the trial at a glance, annotated bibliographies provide both sources for further research and a thorough list of works consulted, a glossary helps students with unfamiliar words and concepts, and a comprehensive index permits quick scanning of the book as a whole.

The insight of Oliver Wendell Holmes Jr., distinguished Supreme Court justice, exemplifies the theme of the *Famous Trials* series. Taken from *The Common Law*, published in 1881, Holmes remarked: "The life of the law has not been logic, it has been experience." That "experience" consists mainly in how laws are applied in society and challenged in the courts, a process resulting in differing outcomes from one generation to the next. Thus, the *Famous Trials* series encourages readers to examine trials within a broader historical and social context.

Introduction

A Thrill Killing

THE ABDUCTION AND murder of a millionaire's son, fourteen-year-old Bobby Franks, which took place only two blocks from his home in Chicago's South Side Kenwood neighborhood on May 21, 1924, alarmed the city. The subsequent arrest of and confessions by two of the victim's wealthy and respected neighbors, Nathan Leopold Jr., aged nineteen, and Richard Loeb, aged eighteen, made the story national and international news. As with the 1999 Columbine High School slaying, argues author Geoffrey Cowan, the Franks murder became a chilling symbol of senseless killing because of the age of those involved. "It captured the nightmare imagination of the country," he said, "because it was so cold-blooded, because it was children killing children."[1]

Even more shocking than the crime itself was the motivation of the perpetrators: the thrill and experience of killing. Further, Franks had been selected virtually at random by Leopold and Loeb. Hal Higdon, an expert on the case and subsequent trial, said that this means of selecting the victim made the crime so infamous. He wrote:

> It was perhaps this single element that elevated their deed to the crime of the century. The sheer randomness of it. The fact that the identity of the victim was decreed by chance, much the way chance dictates which slot on the roulette wheel the ball drops into. As the Franks case eventually became clear, every mother in the city of Chicago would realize that she too had been playing roulette over the life of her son with Leopold and Loeb.[2]

Nathan Leopold Jr. (left) and Richard Loeb kidnapped and murdered fourteen-year-old Bobby Franks. The murder became known as the first "thrill killing" of the twentieth century.

As well as being called the crime of the century, the Franks murder was also known as the first "thrill killing" of the twentieth century and spawned one of the most widely publicized court dramas in American history.

Psychological Testimony

Charged with counts of both kidnapping and murder, both of which carried a maximum sentence of death, Leopold and Loeb were defended by renowned civil rights attorney Clarence Darrow. Faced with the challenge of defending Leopold and Loeb after they had confessed and provided Illinois state's attorney

Robert Crowe an insurmountable amount of evidence of their crime, Darrow knew he could not trust the fates of his clients to a jury. Instead, he threw their lives upon the mercy of the court, headed by Chief Justice John R. Caverly of the Cook County Criminal Court.

By pleading Leopold and Loeb guilty with mitigating circumstances, Darrow entrusted the fate of his clients to Caverly alone. Further, Darrow would present testimony by a panel of expert witnesses from the relatively new field of psychiatry to mitigate (lessen) the sentence of his clients. He hoped to show that although they were not legally insane, Leopold and Loeb had mental diseases that led them to commit their crime. This strategy set important legal precedents, as psychological testimony had never before been used to mitigate a sentence. Caverly's decision to hear such testimony gave new credence to psychological evidence and the validity of its use beyond the conventional limitations of proving or disproving legal insanity.

Impact

The case also became a historic landmark of jurisprudence because it provided Clarence Darrow a platform from which he argued against his long-standing enemy, the death penalty. In a speech that has become a classic of legal oratory, Darrow railed against the death penalty as an ugly remnant of a barbarous and primitive past. While Darrow had already established himself as an important legal figure, this speech secured his position as the best known—and, to many, the best—attorney of the century.

Many argue that the crime and hearing had more of an impact on popular culture than the legal system. The case inspired several books, films, and plays. Most of all it inscribed the names of its two wealthy, intelligent, and debonair defendants, Leopold and Loeb, into history as two of the first American criminal celebrities.

Chapter 1

Kidnapping in Kenwood

O N THURSDAY, MAY 22, 1924, a man walking along the shore of Wolf Lake on the border of Illinois and Indiana discovered the naked body of a young boy in a drainage ditch. The deceased was soon identified as fourteen-year-old Bobby Franks, the son of a Chicago millionaire. The boy had been kidnapped the previous afternoon on his way home from school. The kidnapping had become a homicide—a crime that would lead to one of the most publicized criminal investigations and trials of the twentieth century.

Kenwood

The kidnapping and murder of Bobby Franks became notorious for a number of reasons, among them the fact that Franks was a member of one of Chicago's wealthiest families. The Franks family lived in Kenwood, a then-prestigious and affluent neighborhood on Chicago's South Side, which bordered scenic Lake Shore Drive along the southwestern edge of Lake Michigan near Jackson Park, Hyde Park, and the University of Chicago.

Originally a suburb of Chicago, Kenwood was a residential neighborhood containing many large mid–to-late-nineteenth-century mansions built by some of America's most prominent architects. Primarily wealthy Jewish families of German-American descent, some of whom had been in the neighborhood for generations, populated the district. Among its residents were many of Chicago's most successful Jewish business magnates.

10

Jacob Franks was one such man. He was a successful real estate businessman who by 1924 had made a fortune estimated at $4 million, making him among the wealthiest men in the neighborhood. He, his wife Flora, and their three children— Josephine, seventeen, Jack, fifteen, and Robert (called Bobby), fourteen, lived in a large mansion at the corner of Ellis Avenue and East Fifty-first Street. Although many of the richest families in Chicago customarily resided in the even more affluent north Chicago suburbs, Franks and his family remained in Kenwood so that his sons Jack and Bobby could finish their education at the neighborhood's well-respected prep school, the Harvard School.

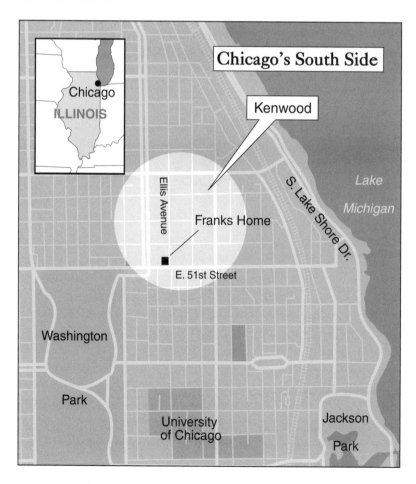

At the Harvard School the Franks's youngest, Bobby, was well liked. He was a good student, active on the debate team, and he frequently participated in after-school athletics. His teachers considered him a brilliant student with a promising future.

On a Normal Wednesday

On Wednesday, May 21, 1924, Bobby Franks attended school as usual. Since the family lived only three city blocks from the Harvard School, he came home at noon to have lunch with his mother as he did every day. He then returned to school at 1 P.M.

After classes ended at 2:30 P.M., Bobby remained at school for two and a half hours while he umpired a baseball game in the schoolyard. When the game was over he left the schoolyard and walked south on Ellis Avenue toward home. Few other people were on the street at the time; however, a young neighborhood boy, nine-year-old Irving Hartman Jr., was walking nearby and noticed Franks.

Only a few moments after Franks left the schoolyard, a car drove north on Ellis, passing the two boys. It made a left onto a side street, turned around, and approached again, this time heading south. As the car slowed to a stop near Franks, Hartman stopped to look at some tulips growing in a yard along the street. When he looked up, Franks was no longer on the sidewalk and the car was racing south on Ellis. Hartman had not seen Franks get into the car and did not think much of the event at the time, but it was the last time anyone would see Franks alive.

Disappeared

That evening Jacob and Flora Franks waited for their son to return from school so they could have supper. By 6:30 P.M., when Bobby had still not returned home, they grew concerned because he had not told anyone in the family of any plans other than the baseball game after school, and it was unlike him to be late. Jacob Franks looked for his son outside on the street while Flora called several of his friends, but he was nowhere to be found, and none of his friends had seen him since he left school after the game. By 7:30 P.M. there was still no sign of their son.

Although the Frankses were anxious, they resolved that Bobby would show up soon with some explanation, and so they ate their evening meal without him.

After supper, the Frankses grew increasingly concerned as time passed. Finally, not knowing what else to do, Jacob Franks called a family friend, attorney Samuel A. Ettelson, for advice. Ettelson said he would come to the house.

Shock

When Ettelson arrived at the Franks house around 9 P.M. there was still no word of Bobby. Jacob and Flora Franks were extremely worried. Ettelson suggested that he and Franks check the school to see if Bobby somehow had been locked in after hours. They contacted R.P. Williams, the school's athletics instructor, who met them at the school and unlocked the building. However, Bobby was not there.

While Franks and Ettelson were searching the Harvard School, the telephone at the Franks home rang. Hoping it was her son, Flora Franks rushed to the telephone and answered it. When she picked it up, however, it was not Bobby but a man whose voice she had never heard before. He said his name was Johnson and told her that Bobby had been kidnapped. "He is all right," he added. "You will receive further news in the morning,"[3] He then hung up.

When Jacob Franks and Ettelson returned from searching the Harvard School, they discovered Flora Franks on the floor, unconscious, having fainted from shock of the news. When she came to her senses, she told her husband about the telephone call. Greatly upset, Franks did not know what they should do. He and Ettelson discussed their options, one of which was to call the police. They decided not to, however, deciding it would be safer for Bobby if they waited for further information from the kidnappers.

By 2 A.M. the kidnappers had not called. Desperate, Franks decided he had to do something, so he and Ettelson drove to the local police precinct where they spoke with the commanding officer on duty. After discussing the matter with the officer,

Franks decided to wait until morning before filing an official report, fearing that if he got the police involved that some harm might come to his son. Instead, he returned home and stayed awake through the night, waiting by the telephone.

AN EXCITING AND WILD ERA

In his seminal book, *Leopold and Loeb: Crime of the Century*, author Hal Higdon describes the excitement and decadence of 1924 Chicago as a social backdrop for the Leopold and Loeb crime and case:

> [It] was a heady time to be young, a time when old taboos and traditions were being swept aside by the shock troops of "flaming youth," who guzzled bathtub gin from hip flasks at their notorious "petting parties." Women, recently given the right to vote, asserted themselves, wearing even-shorter skirts; rolling their stockings below their knees, painting themselves with rouge and lipstick, bobbing their hair, smoking. The flapper was born. . . .
>
> Sex, long a forbidden subject, became a national obsession. . . . It was a time of fads: Mah-Jongg, marathon dancing, six-day bicycle racing, the crossword puzzle craze. Radio, first used commercially four years earlier, had begun to take hold. It was also a time of disrespect for the law because of the Eighteenth Amendment banning liquor. Jack Dempsey ruled as heavyweight champion of the world. Bobby Jones dominated golf. Babe Ruth slugged more home runs. Johnny Weissmuller seemingly broke a new swimming record every weekend. Bill Tilden beat all rivals in tennis. And it was a time of increasing prosperity—Coolidge prosperity—as the country waxed fat under the frugal, honest, laconic, and immobile President Calvin Coolidge.

Two women dance the Charleston on the roof of a Chicago hotel in 1926.

Body at Wolf Lake

At about 7 A.M. the next morning, Thursday, May 22, 1924, Tony Mankowski, a Polish immigrant living near the Indiana/Illinois border, set out on a several-mile walk toward southeastern Chicago to pick up a watch he had left for repair in town. His route took him along the shore of Wolf Lake, a small body of water located on part of a wildlife preserve. As he walked, Mankowski happened to glance down the slope of a culvert where a drainage channel connected Wolf Lake to the adjacent Hyde Lake. Something caught his eye. He stopped and looked more carefully, shocked by what he saw: There appeared to be two bare human feet protruding from a drainage pipe below.

Mankowski saw a railroad crew approaching on a handcar on some nearby railroad tracks, and he flagged them down. He pointed below to what he had seen. The lead crewman, Paul Korff, looked down and exclaimed, "My God. . . . It looks like somebody drowned!"[4] The five men moved down the embankment to the pipe, drew the body out, and laid it on dry ground. Turning it over, they saw that it was the body of a young boy. He was unclothed and clearly dead.

The men brought the body up out of the culvert and took a better look at the boy. They believed that the boy had gone swimming in the lake and had drowned. They looked around for the boy's clothes, but could find only one woolen kneesock. Then, Korff looked down and saw a pair of eyeglasses on the ground. They were small, as if made for a child, with horn-rimmed frames. Korff put them into his pocket to turn over to the police.

The men decided to take the body to the police, so they wrapped it in a tarpaulin and loaded it onto the handcar. With Mankowski, they set off toward Chicago.

Ransom Letter

At about the same time Mankowski and the railroad men discovered the body at Wolf Lake, a special-delivery letter arrived at the

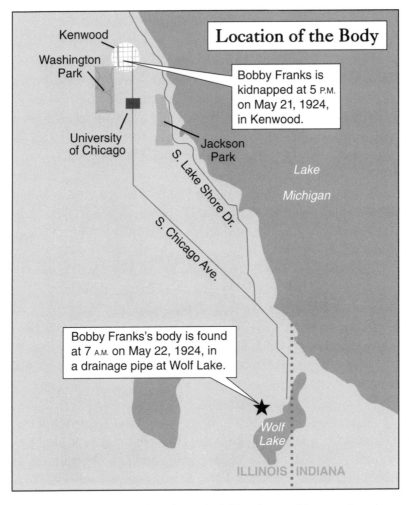

Kenwood

Washington Park

Location of the Body

Bobby Franks is kidnapped at 5 P.M. on May 21, 1924, in Kenwood.

University of Chicago

Jackson Park

S. Lake Shore Dr.

S. Chicago Ave.

Lake

Michigan

Bobby Franks's body is found at 7 A.M. on May 22, 1924, in a drainage pipe at Wolf Lake.

Wolf Lake

ILLINOIS : INDIANA

Franks home. Fatigued and worried, Franks read it, growing more alarmed as he did. The letter's contents confirmed that his son had been kidnapped and gave him instructions to follow. It read:

Dear Sir:

As you no doubt know by this time, your son has been kidnapped. Allow us to assure you that he is at present well and safe. You need fear no physical harm for him, providing you live up carefully to the following instructions, and such others as you will receive by future communications. Should you, however, disobey any of our instructions, even slightly, death will be the penalty.[5]

The letter continued with instructions to gather ten thousand dollars in cash by 1 P.M. that day and to await further instructions. It concluded with a chilling warning: "[W]e are prepared to put our threats into execution, should we have reasonable ground to believe that you have committed an infraction of the above instructions."[6] The letter was signed George Johnson.

Franks called Ettelson and showed him the letter. Ettelson later recalled how it frightened all of them. He said, "Its deliberate tone struck terror into our hearts."[7] Franks asked Ettelson what he thought would be the best thing to do. They agreed that it was best to do what the kidnappers said to ensure the boy's safe return, so Ettelson recommended that Franks go to the bank to collect the money.

A Tragic Connection

Later that morning the city editor of the *Chicago Daily News* was given a lead about a possible kidnapping. An anonymous caller had told him that attorney Sam Ettelson had information about it, so he telephoned reporter James Mulroy and instructed him to go to Ettelson's office to question the attorney.

When Mulroy arrived at Ettelson's office, the attorney denied any knowledge of the crime. However, when it was clear that the reporter was going to pursue the story and perhaps endanger the ransom plans, Ettelson admitted he had information. He made a deal that he would tell Mulroy what he knew if the reporter promised to wait on the story until the ransom drop had been made. Mulroy agreed. Ettelson filled him in on the details, and then the two men went to the Franks home to await further development.

Soon afterward the *Daily News* city editor learned that the apparently drowned body of a young boy had been discovered at Wolf Lake that morning and had been taken to a funeral home morgue for autopsy. The editor assigned reporter Alvin Goldstein to the story. Goldstein went to the funeral home and

A man points to the spot near Wolf Lake where Bobby Franks's body was found. The body had been stuffed headfirst into a drainage pipe.

returned with his story, including a description of the victim's body, for the afternoon edition.

From the description of the apparent drowning victim, the *Daily News* city editor had a hunch that the drowning and kidnapping stories might be connected. He called Goldstein. "From what we know, it might be the kid,"[8] said the editor. He instructed the reporter to call Mulroy and give Jacob Franks the description of the body found at Wolf Lake to see if it fit his son.

Goldstein described the boy as about five feet tall and weighing about one hundred pounds. Police presumed the glasses found near the body belonged to the boy, so Goldstein included them in the description. Jacob Franks said it was not his son. As one reporter for the *Chicago Daily News* wrote, "It did seem a little preposterous to suppose that the body in the morgue was that of Bobby Franks."[9] Bobby was older and, most important, he did not wear glasses. Nonetheless, Jacob Franks asked his brother-in-law Edwin Gresham to go to the morgue just in case.

A STRICTLY COMMERCIAL PROPOSITION

The ransom letter Jacob Franks received on the morning of Thursday, May 22, 1924, contained specific and detailed instructions to follow. Reprinted in the May 23, 1924, edition of the *Chicago Times*, according to attorney Samuel Ettelson, "Its deliberate tone struck terror into our hearts."

Dear Sir:

As you no doubt know by this time, your son has been kidnapped. Allow us to assure you that he is at present well and safe. You need fear no physical harm for him, providing you live up carefully to the following instructions, and such others as you will receive by future communications. Should you, however, disobey any of our instructions, even slightly, death will be the penalty.

For obvious reasons, make absolutely no attempt to communicate with either the police authorities or any private agency. Should you already have communicated with the police, allow them to continue their investigations, but do not mention this letter.

Secure, before noon today, $10,000.00. This money must be composed entirely of old bills, of the following denominations: $2,000.00 in $20.00 bills; $8,000.00 in $50.00 bills. The money must be old. Any attempt to include new or marked bills will render the entire venture futile. The money should be placed in a large cigar box, or if such is impossible, in a heavy cardboard box, securely closed and wrapped in white paper. The wrapping paper should be sealed at all openings with sealing wax.

Have the money thus prepared as directed above, and remain home after one o'clock p.m. See that the telephone is not in use.

You will receive further communication instructing you as to your future course. As a final word of warning, this is a strictly commercial proposition, and we are prepared to put our threats into execution, should we have reasonable ground to believe that you have committed an infraction of the above instructions. However, should you carefully follow our instructions to the letter, we can assure you that your son will be safely returned to you within six hours of our receipt of the money.

Yours truly,

George Johnson.

A Close Call

A little after 3 P.M. the Franks's telephone rang, and Ettelson answered. The person on the other end of the line identified himself as the kidnapper, George Johnson. He said that he was sending a taxicab that Franks was to take, and he supplied an address. Ettelson asked him to repeat himself and handed the telephone to Franks. The kidnapper said again: "A taxi cab will be at your door."[10] He told Franks to take the cab to a drugstore on East Sixty-third Street and gave him the address. Franks asked if he could have more time, but Johnson said no and hung up.

When Franks put down the telephone, he realized that he was so distracted and nervous that he could not remember the address the kidnapper had given. Neither could Ettelson. They both panicked. The telephone rang again. Franks picked it up, hoping it was the kidnapper again, but it was his brother-in-law, Gresham, calling from the funeral home. He had bad news. The body found at Wolf Lake that morning was indeed Bobby's.

Confusion and Disbelief

Jacob and Flora Franks were in shock from the news. It did not make sense that the body at the morgue could be Bobby. Why would the kidnapper kill him before even receiving the ransom? Flora Franks refused to believe it. A few minutes later a cab-driver arrived at the Franks house. Ettelson interrogated the driver, hoping for information that would lead them to the person responsible. "Who sent for you?" he demanded, "Where are you supposed to go?"[11] However, the driver knew nothing. He had merely responded to a call from someone claiming to be Jacob Franks needing a taxi. He did not know the destination. The driver was paid for his trouble and he left.

The news spread quickly through the neighborhood, and by the afternoon, papers announced the news to the city that the millionaire's son Bobby Franks had been murdered and left unclothed and beaten in a drainage pipe. People all over the city responded with shock and alarm. Author Maureen McKernan wrote, "Wild rumors swept the town. Almost every detective on the force was assigned to the case. Every newspaper in town assigned its best reporters to the story."[12] The largest manhunt in Chicago's history began before the day was done.

Chapter 2

Manhunt

WHILE MURDER WAS a daily and almost commonplace occurrence in Chicago in 1924, the murder of Bobby Franks was a special case. In the days that followed the discovery of Frank's body, the crime received unprecedented media attention, as it inspired the largest, most aggressive, and most publicized manhunt and criminal investigation in the history of Chicago at that time.

A Compelling Crime

Of the hundreds of wrongful deaths in Chicago each year during the 1920s, few received the publicity and police attention that the Bobby Franks murder did. The Franks case was of special interest to many because the victim was young and from a wealthy family, and because his body had been dumped naked after having suffered what appeared to be a brutal assault.

According to historian Scott A. Newman, the fact that a child from an affluent family had not only been kidnapped but also ruthlessly—and seemingly senselessly—murdered shocked many people who believed that wealth ensured against such tragedy. "[The crime] seemed to give lie to the founding premise of [upper] middle-class life: that hard work and moral behavior were their own rewards and thus the key to lifelong happiness."[13] Additionally, the condition of the body suggested that the killer or killers might have sexually assaulted and/or tortured Franks.

Such a crime was a boon for the publishers of Chicago's newspapers. The newspaper business in Chicago during the 1920s was an extremely competitive and sometimes unethical

21

NEW BRIGHTON HIGH SCHOOL
NEW BRIGHTON. PA 15066

industry, often relying on sensationalism and unscrupulous journalism to attract readers. Many newspaper editors and journalists ruthlessly exploited tragedy to sell more copies of their papers, and the Franks case was no exception. Police soon felt the pressure of an outraged public demanding swift apprehension of the criminals responsible for the crime.

Evidence

However, police had few leads with which to begin their investigation. The only physical evidence of the crime other than Franks's body was the ransom letter and the pair of small horn-rimmed glasses that had been found near the body. Police now knew the glasses did not belong to the boy, and they believed that they might belong to the killer.

Investigators followed up on these two leads thoroughly. Although they were not optimistic about finding the owner of the glasses since the frames were a common style and the lenses were a common prescription, police urged Chicago opticians to check their records for sales of such pairs. They also released a photograph of the glasses to newspapers to enlist public assistance in identifying their owner.

The only evidence found near Bobby Franks's body was a pair of glasses. Newspapers published a photo of the glasses hoping the public could identify their owner.

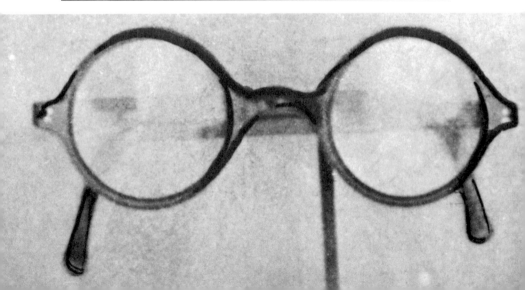

Police also brought in experts in type analysis to examine the ransom letter. The results showed that it had been typed on a portable (manual) Underwood typewriter and that the handwritten address on the envelope suggested someone purposefully wrote messily to disguise his or her penmanship.

The coroner's office also examined the ransom letter. Coroner Oscar Wolff said the writer's proficiency in English suggested he was educated and dangerous. He said: "[The letter] would signify intelligence, a dangerous attribute in a criminal. . . . Greed would be the controlling passion, and, dead or alive, they intended to cash in on Robert Franks, the millionaire's son."[14]

The third element of physical evidence in the case was Franks's body. On May 22 the Chicago coroner's office held an investigation into the cause of death. An autopsy revealed Franks had died from a combination of two blows with a blunt object to the skull and suffocation.

Superficial scratches all over the back of Franks's body suggested that it had been dragged along the ground at some point, and ruptured blood vessels indicated that he had struggled against his attacker. There was discoloration on the face, hands, and genitals caused by some sort of corrosive liquid. The autopsy showed no evidence of sexual abuse, which had been a suspicion of police since Franks had been found naked.

A Desperate Search

Public pressure to catch the killers mounted as days passed. In response, hundreds of police officers fielded and investigated dozens of tips about the crime, but all proved to be hoaxes, mistakes, or otherwise useless. The only suspects that had been promising were three teachers from the Harvard School, but the men had to be released when sufficient evidence against them could not be found.

In desperation, police began sweeping the city, arresting all known sex offenders and drug addicts for interrogation. Further, anyone caught in any kind of suspicious circumstance was arrested and questioned. Police even took leads from a psychic from Kansas who claimed to have had a vision of the crime.

Despite police efforts none of the strategies worked, and the possibility of catching the killer seemed increasingly hopeless. However, on Thursday, May 29, police got a break in the case.

Breakthrough

Earlier in the week, on Sunday, May 25, police had questioned Nathan Leopold Jr. Leopold was a nineteen-year-old University of Chicago graduate, law student, and amateur ornithologist. He frequently visited the Wolf Lake area on a regular basis to study birds. He came from a wealthy Kenwood neighborhood family who lived only blocks away from the Frankses and admitted to having been

PRIME SUSPECTS

Following the identification of Bobby Franks's body, State's Attorney Crowe and the Chicago police chief pressed investigators to come up with suspects as soon as possible. On Saturday, May 24, police arrested their first suspects in the case, all of them teachers at the Harvard School about whom students or fellow teachers had suspicions. They were R.P. Williams, who taught athletics; Walter Wilson, a mathematics teacher; and Mott Kirk Mitchell, an English teacher at the Harvard School whom police suspected of being a homosexual and whom several current and former students accused of having sexually propositioned them.

Police brought the men in for questioning. Williams was released within hours because at the time Franks was kidnapped he had been walking another student home from school. Mitchell and Wilson, however, were held for six days of continual interrogation.

In their zeal to find the killer of Bobby Franks, police reportedly beat and threatened their suspects. Wilson claimed that police had hit him repeatedly with a rubber hose and threatened to kill him unless he confessed. Mitchell eventually confessed to sexually molesting several Harvard School students during his teaching career but maintained his innocence in the Franks case.

On May 28, Wilson and Williams's attorneys successfully issued a writ of habeus corpus in court, which required that the police charge the men with a crime or release them. Without evidence to keep them in custody, State's Attorney Crowe let them go, although police continued to follow them, hoping to uncover some evidence to implicate either in the crime. No such evidence ever surfaced. Mitchell never returned to teaching at the Harvard School and Wilson left the city for months before returning to his job.

Police questioned Nathan Leopold Jr. early in their investigation but dismissed him as an unlikely suspect.

in the area the weekend before the body was found. Because of Leopold's wealth, status, and easy demeanor, the police doubted that the young man had anything to do with the crime, so they took his statement and released him.

Meanwhile, as Chicago opticians searched their records to find the owner of the horn-rimmed glasses, optician Almer Coe discovered that the frames were fitted with an unusual hinge. His business was the only one in Chicago carrying frames with such a hinge. On Thursday, May 29, after a week of hand-checking his company's records of over fifty-four thousand pairs of glasses sold over the years, Coe told police that he had sold only three pairs of such frames. The owners of the special frames were an attorney traveling in Europe, a woman who still had her pair, and Nathan F. Leopold Jr., the young man from Kenwood whom police had interviewed days earlier.

Leopold Questioned

The lead was promising. However, as police had, State's Attorney Crowe at first doubted that Leopold was involved with the crime because of his family's reputation and affluence. Aware that police attention might arouse the press and damage the Leopold family's reputation, Crowe summoned Leopold to a suite at the La Salle Hotel instead of to the police station. Leopold was picked up Thursday in the early afternoon.

When questioned about the glasses Leopold denied owner-ship. "If I were not positive that my glasses are at home, I would say these are mine."[15] However, when a search of his home failed to turn up his own pair, he admitted they must be his. He said that he had probably stumbled and dropped them on a birding expedition the weekend before Franks was murdered. He said he had not noticed them missing because he rarely wore them and kept them in his poorest suit, which he used only for birding.

Although the story sounded plausible, Crowe's suspicions were aroused when Leopold could not get the glasses to fall from

his pocket when he reen-acted stumbling in front of investigators. Crowe asked Leopold to tell him where he had been the afternoon and evening of Wednesday, May 21, the day of the Franks murder. Leopold said he could not recall, but Crowe and other investigators con-tinued pressing him to remember. After much questioning Leopold fi-nally admitted that he was reluctant to tell the details of the day because the story involved a close friend, Richard Loeb.

Richard Loeb's alibi aroused suspicion with police because it differed significantly from Leopold's.

Leopold said he did not want police to bother Loeb because of him. Nevertheless, Leopold gave his alibi for the afternoon and evening of the crime.

Alibi

Leopold said that he and Richard Loeb had spent the afternoon at a park, picnicking in Leopold's car, drinking liquor. They then went to dinner at a Chinese restaurant near the University of Chicago. Afterward, they cruised around nearby Lincoln Park in his car looking for girls. He and Loeb had picked up two young women, named Edna and Mae, and had driven somewhere near the park with them. He said they had intended to seduce the women, but when the women refused, Leopold and Loeb kicked them out of the car. After that, he had driven Loeb home and then gone home himself.

Investigators thought the alibi seemed implausible but possible. They asked him to repeat his alibi several times, asking for more details. They also questioned him about his personal life, his background, and his education. Although police questioned him for hours in hope of upsetting or flustering him so that he would reveal something incriminating, Leopold answered politely and calmly throughout the interrogation. It was almost 4 A.M. Friday morning before they stopped to let him rest.

Thursday evening, shortly after Leopold told his alibi to police, officers picked up Richard Loeb and brought him to a separate room of the La Salle Hotel to confirm Leopold's story. Like Leopold, Loeb initially claimed he could not clearly remember his whereabouts on the day of the crime. However, investigators refused to accept his answer and pressed him until he finally said that he had spent the afternoon with Leopold and then had gone home for the evening, which he spent alone. He did not refer to cruising or to Edna and Mae. The difference between the two men's stories made investigators very suspicious. Loeb was also interrogated through the night. Afterward, Crowe had both men taken to the police station jail for a few hours of rest before they would be questioned further.

Speaking to the Press

Because of their families' wealth and status in the community, Leopold and Loeb were treated politely by police and even allowed to speak separately to the press on Friday morning while still under arrest. Leopold was magnanimous toward police when he gave a statement to reporters. "I don't blame police for holding me," he said. "I'm sorry this happened only because it will worry my family. But I'll certainly be glad to do the best I can to help [the] police."[16]

One of the reporters who interviewed them was Loeb's friend Howard Mayer. Mayer could not believe that his friends could be involved in the crime, but police told him that they were under suspicion because their alibis did not match. When Mayer visited Leopold he told him this news. Leopold showed concern and pleaded with Mayer to speak to Loeb on his behalf. "Tell him to remember what happened on Wednesday," he implored. "He'll understand."[17]

Believing he was simply conveying a message between friends, Mayer privately told Loeb what Leopold had said. Loeb thanked Mayer and asked to speak to the police again. When investigators returned, Loeb told them that he now remembered more clearly the events of May 21. He then told them a story similar to the one that Leopold had, including the details of picking up Edna and Mae.

Another Link to Leopold

While police continued interrogating Leopold and Loeb, on Friday, May 30, reporters Mulroy and Goldstein continued investigating the case for the *Daily News*. They interviewed Arnold Maremont, one of Leopold's classmates at the University of Chicago Law School. Maremont said that Leopold frequently typed up study sheets for a study group to which he, Leopold, and a few other University of Chicago students belonged. Maremont showed the reporters several study sheets, and Goldstein noticed that one of the documents had been typed on a different machine than the rest. The type looked like that of an Underwood, the

State's Attorney Robert Crowe (left) and investigators examine the typewriter used to type the ransom letter. The typewriter was found in Jackson Park.

same machine used to write the ransom letter to Jacob Franks. Maremont agreed, saying that he recalled noticing a portable Underwood typewriter in the Leopold library a few months before.

The reporters had a typewriter specialist examine the study sheet. The expert confirmed that not only had the document been typed on an Underwood but also on the same Underwood that had been used in the kidnapping letter. They immediately reported their findings to State's Attorney Crowe.

Upon hearing the news Crowe called the students from Leopold's study group together and interviewed them in Leopold's presence. Each student claimed to having seen an Underwood typewriter at Leopold's house a few weeks ago. Confronted with this information, Leopold steadfastly denied that he had ever owned an Underwood. He suggested it might have belonged to a friend of his, Leon Mandel, who was traveling in Europe at the time and could not be reached to confirm the information.

Police interviewed the staff of the Leopold household about the typewriter. The maid, Elizabeth Sattler, said that she had seen an Underwood in Leopold's rooms several times in the past months. However, she had not seen it recently, and a search of the house failed to produce the Underwood.

Frustration and Doubt

By Friday afternoon State's Attorney Crowe was frustrated. There was now significant doubt as to whether he had the right men. Even if he had been sure that Leopold and Loeb were the killers, the evidence regarding the glasses and the typewriter was all circumstantial and insufficient to go to court with. Leopold could have lost his glasses on a birding expedition, and the Underwood typewriter had disappeared. Further, the two men's alibis for the day of the crime now matched.

Crowe realized that without hard evidence he would have to let them go. Their status and wealth made it impossible for him to do otherwise. He said to his staff, "They've got wealthy parents. We've got to either book them or release them."[18] He set a deadline for midnight that night. If substantial evidence against the men did not turn up before that time, he would let them go.

Conclusive Evidence

As the hours ran out, the lead case investigator under Crowe, Bert Cronson, decided he wanted to interview the Leopold family chauffeur Sven Englund to confirm Leopold's alibi. Cronson questioned Englund a little while before midnight. To Cronson's surprise, when asked about the day of the crime Englund revealed that Leopold had left his car—a red Winton Willys-Knight touring car—at home all afternoon the day of the kidnapping and murder. Leopold had asked Englund to make some repairs on the car's brakes. Cronson asked if he was sure because,

THE GREY GHOST

An early lead in the Franks murder investigation came from the eyewitness statement of Irving Hartman Jr., the boy who had been on the street near Bobby Franks the afternoon he disappeared. Hartman was able to describe the vehicle he had seen racing away after Franks had vanished, including that it was a Winton, a popular make of car at the time. This identification was backed up by a chauffeur to one of the neighborhood families who had seen a dirty gray Winton near the Harvard School the day before the kidnapping, as well as early the day Franks disappeared.

Police released the description of a 1922–1924 gray Winton to the press, asking for people to come forward with information. They soon received several reports of sightings of vehicles fitting the car's description. Although none of the leads was enough to determine the ownership or destination of the automobile, police still considered the car their most promising lead. Drivers of gray Wintons in Chicago were questioned. However, the strategy failed, as none appeared to be involved with the crime.

Sitting in the car used in the crime, Loeb talks with State's Attorney Crowe. After confessing, Leopold and Loeb led police to the car.

if so, Leopold and Loeb's alibis about picking up girls in his car had to be a lie.

Englund said he could prove it. His daughter had been sick that day and he had picked up a prescription for her at the pharmacy. The bottle would have the date on it. Englund returned home for the bottle. When he returned he showed it to Cronson. The date on the label read May 21, 1924, the day Bobby Franks had been kidnapped and killed. Cronson gave the information to Crowe just before the deadline ran out. Crowe was thrilled. He exclaimed, "I think we've got them!"[19]

The Confessions

Shortly after midnight on Saturday, May 31, 1924, armed with the evidence provided by Englund, Crowe instructed his men to intensify their questioning of Leopold and Loeb. John Sbarbaro, who questioned Loeb, urged the young man to confess for the sake of his conscience. He said the police knew he was lying and that Leopold's car had been in the garage all afternoon. Hearing this, Loeb's face turned ashen and he trembled. "My God," Loeb cried, "can that be true?"[20]

Defeated, Loeb asked to see Crowe, and then, beginning at 1:40 A.M., he delivered a full confession in the presence of a court reporter. In his confession Loeb claimed the crime had been Leopold's idea and that Leopold had been the one who actually murdered the boy. He said: "I am fully convinced that neither the idea nor the act would have occurred to me had it not been for the suggestion and stimulus of Leopold. Furthermore, I do not believe that I would have been capable of having killed Franks."[21]

Crowe then confronted Leopold, telling him that he could stop lying now. "Your pal has just confessed, told us the whole story," he said. Leopold thought Crowe was bluffing. "Do you think I'm stupid?" he said. "I'm not going to believe that. Anyhow, it's impossible. There's nothing to confess."[22]

However, Crowe then provided him with numerous details of the crime that he had gotten from Loeb's confession—details only the two men could have known. Leopold realized that his friend had confessed. Worse, Crowe revealed that Loeb had also said that Leopold had been the one responsible for the idea for the crime and the actual murder. Leopold became angry. He realized his friend and accomplice had not only given in but had also betrayed him. He said to Crowe that he would tell the real story.

Crowe called in the court reporter, and Leopold began his confession. During the confession, Crowe noted that details were strikingly similar to Loeb's confession with the exception that Leopold said that Loeb, not he, had committed the actual murder.

Betrayal

Leopold's statement concluded at 4:20 A.M. on Saturday morning, May 31. Following that, the two men were then brought into a room together where their confessions were read back to them by the court reporter. Leopold and Loeb sat staring angrily at each other throughout. Each maintained that the other was responsible for the planning of their crime and of actually killing Franks.

At one point during the reading of Loeb's comment, an argument between the two broke out regarding Loeb's testimony. When Crowe asked who had wrapped the chisel that was used as the murder weapon, Loeb pointed to Leopold and said that he had. When Leopold objected, Loeb said: "I tried to help you out, which is more than you would have done for me because I thought if worst came to worst you would admit what you had done."[23] Leopold called him a liar. "Those are all absurd, dirty lies. He is trying to get out of this mess."[24]

However, it did not make a difference whether or not they agreed. According to the law, both of them could be tried for kidnapping and murder.

Scavenger Hunt

Later that morning, with a transcript of their confessions in hand, Crowe made a statement to reporters. "The Franks murder mystery has been solved,"[25] he said. He added that he had received full confessions from Leopold and Loeb.

Soon afterward Crowe and his team of investigators took Leopold and Loeb on a tour of points of importance to their

Police search a field near the Indiana border for Franks's shoes and belt. Leopold and Loeb led police to several sites where they had disposed of evidence.

crime. The accused traveled with detectives and some reporters that Crowe had selected. Leopold and Loeb rode in separate cars since the once close friends now refused contact with each other.

Among the sites the tour visited were the car rental agency where Leopold had obtained the blue Willys-Knight for their crime; the hardware store where the chisel had been purchased; the drugstore where Leopold had purchased the hydrochloric acid the men had used on their victim to hinder identification of the body; and Jackson Park, where they had disposed of the Underwood typewriter a few days after their crime. They also went to the Indiana border where Leopold claimed that he and Loeb had thrown out Franks's shoes and belt.

Leopold was particularly talkative during the ride, enjoying the attention. He bragged about how much planning had gone into the crime. When asked why he committed the crime, he replied, "It was just an experiment. It is as easy for us to justify as an entomologist in impaling a beetle on a pin."[26]

A Hanging Case

After all the evidence was collected, Leopold and Loeb were put into a hotel and guarded while they slept. Crowe held a press conference where he announced that he had enough evidence to corroborate the confessions of Leopold and Loeb and that he could go to court immediately if he had to. He also announced that the state would prosecute the men to the fullest extent of the law, which for the crime of first degree homicide was death by hanging. "I have a hanging case," he said, "and I would be willing to submit it to a jury tomorrow."[27] However, the Leopold and Loeb families had already taken steps to protect the accused men.

Chapter 3

A Perfect Crime

IN THEIR CONFESSIONS to State's Attorney Robert Crowe and his staff, Nathan Leopold and Richard Loeb revealed facts about themselves that no other people knew. Most surprising was the revelation that they had developed a secret criminal partnership that had begun when they were fifteen years old and which had climaxed in the kidnapping and murder of Bobby Franks. Further, the Franks murder had been a crime that the two had carefully planned and executed as an amusement and a coldly calculated intellectual exercise.

Backgrounds

During their confessions, Leopold and Loeb provided detailed information about the conception, planning, and execution of the kidnapping and murder of Franks. They also provided background and insight into how their criminal partnership had begun.

Like their victim, Leopold and Loeb came from wealthy Jewish families in Kenwood. Loeb's father was a vice president of Sears, Roebuck and Company with a fortune of over $4 million, and Leopold's was a Chicago manufacturer with a fortune of over $1 million.

Both young men had been precocious children who had become highly intelligent young men, both having been graduated from prestigious South Side preparatory schools far in advance of their peers. (Leopold had graduated from the same prep school, the Harvard School, as their victim, Franks.)

Reputations and Rumors

In their Kenwood neighborhood Leopold and Loeb were known as brilliant and somewhat arrogant young men. Leopold had an IQ of 210, and in addition to being a renowned amateur ornithologist, was an expert linguist who could speak five languages and read ten. Loeb, the more athletic and popular of the pair, also had a high IQ, although not nearly as high as Leopold's.

Leopold and Loeb had met at the University of Chicago when they were fifteen years old. There, they had developed a strong friendship. They transferred schools together in 1922 to the University of Michigan in Ann Arbor where Loeb graduated in 1923

INTELLIGENCE AND CRIME

In her book, *Kidnapped: Child Abduction in America*, Paula S. Fass argues that one of the most disturbing implications of the confessions of Leopold and Loeb was that it destroyed conventional beliefs about criminals' intelligence. She writes,

Leopold and Loeb's confessions upended conventional categories and definitions. Even though beliefs about crime in the 1920s no longer gave much credence to . . . visions of criminals as primitive types, the use of intelligence tests before [World War I] . . . had created an association between crime and subnormal intelligence. This association was strongly challenged in the 1920s by some, like Carl Murchison, who used the same kind of [intelligence] tests . . . to question the relationship between crime and what was called feeblemindedness. "The same characteristics that make for worldly success in business and professional life also make for success in crime," Murchison announced. But Murchison also concluded that "the evidence is very strong that college training is a strong preventive of violence. For all practical purposes, crimes of violence on the part of college men can be ignored." The Murchison connection between intelligence and crime could not quite explain the case of Leopold and Loeb, boys who were not simply smart criminals or juvenile delinquents but highly educated murderers who challenged their society and its definitions to the core. . . . Initially, at least, they seemed to dissolve ordinary categories as they upturned traditional motives.

at eighteen years of age, the youngest graduate in the school's history. Loeb had been a member of the Phi chapter of the prestigious Zeta Beta Tau fraternity at the University of Michigan.

During their friendship at the University of Michigan, there had been rumors that Leopold and Loeb had a sexual relationship. In fact, one of the conditions for Loeb's entering his fraternity had been that he cease his friendship with Leopold. Loeb agreed and shunned Leopold in public. In confessing to the murder of Franks, Loeb denied a homosexual relationship; however, he said that they pretended to stay away from each other for the sake of appearances while still seeing each other secretly. "We were very careful never to go alone together in public, seen together any place, or to be alone any place where we could be seen."[28]

The situation was alleviated when Leopold returned to the University of Chicago in 1922, after his mother's death, and was graduated from there with high honors in 1923. When Loeb returned to Chicago after graduating from the University of Michigan, the two men began spending much of their time together again.

Both men enrolled in postgraduate work at the University of Chicago in preparation for law school, which they planned to attend at different schools in the fall of 1924. However, their promising plans would never be fulfilled because, beneath their outward appearances, they harbored a secret life that would change the direction of their lives and that of Bobby Franks.

Double Lives

Leopold and Loeb had embarked together on a secret life of crime soon after meeting. Wealthy beyond the aspirations of most adult men at the time, Leopold and Loeb committed crimes not for money but for thrills. At first they committed only petty crimes, such as shoplifting, vandalism, and making false alarm fire calls; however, the seriousness of their offenses grew over time as their daring and desire for risk increased. According to one source, "Stealing small objects graduated into stealing and vandalizing cars. Making annoying phone calls to school instructors graduated into turning in false fire alarms which then graduated into arson."[29]

Leopold (left) and Loeb stand trial in Joliet, Illinois, while in prison for the murder of Franks. The men were sued by an Ann Arbor taxi driver who claimed they beat him.

In November 1923 they made a special trip to Ann Arbor to burglarize Loeb's former fraternity house on the University of Michigan campus. Masked and armed with handguns, ready to shoot anyone who caught them in the act, they committed the crime in the middle of the night while residents slept. During this burglary, among the items they stole was a portable Underwood typewriter that would later play a significant role in the criminal investigation of the Franks murder.

The Plan

Soon after the fraternity house burglary, Leopold and Loeb came up with an idea to plan and execute a kidnapping and murder. They would choose someone wealthy and demand ransom of ten thousand dollars from the family after the victim was already dead. It would be their greatest and final crime, something they could look back on with pleasure and satisfaction in their adult lives.

Planning the crime was an exciting intellectual exercise to

Leopold and Loeb. They spent months discussing it in painstaking detail. Over time, their plan took shape: They would abduct the victim in a car, render him or her unconscious, then drive to a remote place where they would kill the victim.

The two decided to use anesthetic as the means of killing their victim, because, Loeb said in his confession, it "would be the easiest way of putting [the victim] to death, and the least messy."[30] They would then disfigure the body to make it difficult to identify and dump it somewhere. Lastly, they would collect ransom from the victim's family using telephone calls and letters to lead them on an elaborate route of taxis and trains to make it difficult for the police to follow. The ransom delivery instructions would include that the money be thrown from a moving train at a specified remote spot where they could pick it up after ensuring that no police were around.

Choosing a Victim

As for the selection of the victim, the two coolly debated for weeks over who would be suitable. At one point they even considered their own fathers and Loeb's younger brother Tommy as candidates. They decided against these possibilities, not out of love or devotion but because they knew that they would be suspects if the victim were related to them. They thought of abducting a woman and raping her as well as murdering her, but Loeb vetoed the idea because he believed women were more closely watched and would be more difficult to abduct. Their final criteria were that the victim should be a child, a member of a wealthy family who could pay a large ransom without hesitation, and someone the two men knew well enough to lure into a car.

With these requirements in mind, they decided to leave the identity of the victim up to fate until the day of the crime. In his confession, Leopold said: "We decided to pick the most likely-looking subject that came our way."[31]

Preparations

The first step in executing the plan required Leopold and Loeb to create a fictitious identity that would allow them to

A CHARACTER STUDY

Soon after the confessions of Leopold and Loeb were announced, many who knew the two accused men were called upon to give their reaction. In this June 2, 1924, excerpt from the *Chicago Daily News*, Lessing Rosenwald, whose son was a friend of Leopold and Loeb's, provides a character study of the men:

"Richard Loeb is a fine fellow, and I can't understand why he would do a thing like that," said Mr. Rosenwald. "If he wanted money all he had to do was ask for it. I don't know Leopold as well, but I do believe he dominated Richard and I suspected he was the influence in this awful affair. . . .

"[Loeb's] father is a very good friend of mine, he practically broke me into the business [Sears, Roebuck & Co.]," said Mr. Rosenwald. "There can be no finer man than Mr. Loeb. I knew Richard as a brother, and I can't believe this thing about him. As for Leopold, I did not know him as well. I know of him, of course. He was considered a genius. When he was 16 years old he had one of the finest collections of butterflies in the world. Eight different departments in Washington would write to him for opinions and he contributed to magazines and has written several books about ornithology. He was the youngest man ever graduated from the University of Chicago, receiving his diploma when 18. Leopold thought he must get experience and the only reason I can conceive for his doing that [the Franks murder] would be that he thought the experience was worth it. He had probably been reading modernistic literature and had obtained this idea of experience from that."

rent a car without the possibility of it being traced back to either of them later. Using the pseudonym Morton D. Ballard, they opened a bank account to establish credit, checked into a hotel to established an address, and then rented a car, using fake personal references.

As Ballard, Leopold rented a blue Winton Willys-Knight touring car (it would be mistaken for gray by eyewitnesses), a car the same make and model as his own, except his was red. He returned it two hours later and had the rental agency issue him a card so that he could easily pick up the same car on the day of their crime without having to provide references again. With this rehearsal complete, Leopold and Loeb set the date for their crime: May 21, 1924, a Wednesday.

The week before the crime, they typed up the ransom letter and letters of instruction they planned to use in the crime, writing them on the Underwood typewriter stolen from Loeb's Zeta Beta Tau fraternity house months earlier. Finally, on Tuesday, May 20, the day before the execution of their plan, Loeb bought a chisel from a hardware store. They wrapped the blade so it could be gripped, allowing the handle to be used as a bludgeon to knock out their victim.

Prowling Kenwood

On the morning of May 21 Leopold and Loeb followed a well-rehearsed schedule. They met on the University of Chicago campus at 11 A.M., after Leopold's classes, and drove his car downtown to the Rent-A-Car agency where Leopold rented the same car as he had rented weeks before. They had lunch and then dropped Leopold's car at his home with the family chauffeur, asking him to fix the brakes, which Leopold said were squeaking. The two then drove the rental car to Jackson Park on the lakefront of Lake Michigan where they parked for an hour.

At 2 P.M. they drove back to Kenwood and parked near the Harvard School and waited for class to let out at 2:30 P.M. Leopold and especially Loeb were well known and trusted by many neighborhood children, so they thought it would be easy to lure a child into the car with the promise of a ride. However, they had to time it right so that no one was around to see their victim get into their car. First, the street remained too crowded immediately after class let out. Then they lost sight of one intended victim when he disappeared onto the playground to join a baseball game. However, they were patient and waited for another victim.

The Offer of a Ride Home

At 5 P.M. Bobby Franks stepped out onto the sidewalk in front of the Harvard School and headed south on Ellis toward home, just as Leopold and Loeb cruised by heading north. Loeb knew Franks, as he was a distant relative and frequently played tennis on courts at the Loeb home. They had their victim.

In their confessions, Leopold and Loeb each described the

preparations and events of the crime with close similarity up to this point. In Leopold's version, he was driving and Loeb committed the actual murder. In Loeb's confession, the details were the same, although his and Leopold's roles in the crime were reversed.

They turned the car around so that they could pull up alongside Franks. Loeb called the boy over to the car and asked if he wanted a ride. Although Franks lived only two blocks away, Loeb persuaded him to get into the car. In his version of the story, Leopold recalled:

> Richard asked Robert if he minded if we took him around the block, to which Robert said no. As soon as we

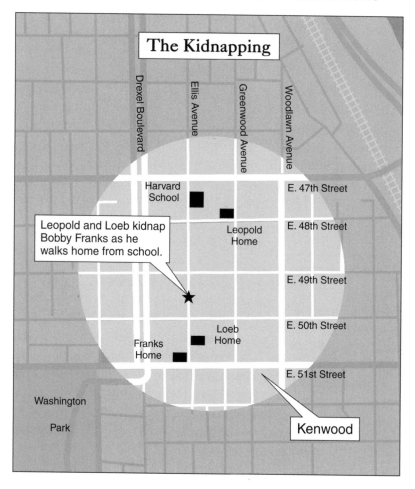

The Kidnapping

Drexel Boulevard
Ellis Avenue
Greenwood Avenue
Woodlawn Avenue

Harvard School

E. 47th Street

Leopold and Loeb kidnap Bobby Franks as he walks home from school.

Leopold Home

E. 48th Street

E. 49th Street

Loeb Home

E. 50th Street

Franks Home

E. 51st Street

Washington

Park

Kenwood

turned the corner, Richard placed his hand over Robert's mouth to stifle his outcry, with his right hand beating him on the head several times with a chisel, especially prepared for the purpose. The boy did not succumb as readily as we had believed so for fear of being observed Richard seized him, and pulled him into the back seat. Here he forced a cloth into his mouth. Apparently the boy died instantly by suffocation shortly there after.[32]

Disposing of the Evidence

After killing Franks, Leopold and Loeb drove south toward the Illinois/Indiana state border with the boy on the floorboards of the back seat, wrapped in an auto robe. They had to waste some time before darkness fell, so they stopped at a roadside food stand and ate supper in the car. Once it was dark, they drove to Wolf Lake where Leopold knew there was a drainage pipe in which they could hide the body. They disrobed Franks and then poured hydrochloric acid on his face and body to make identification more difficult. Loeb later said: "We knew he was dead, by the fact that rigor mortis had set in, and also by his eyes, and then when at that same time we poured this hydrochloric acid over him, we noticed no tremor, not a single tremor in his body, therefore we were sure he was dead."[33]

Dressed in hip boots that he used to bird, Leopold climbed into the culvert with the body and pushed it into the pipe, face down. The two then gathered Franks's clothing and carried it back to the car. At this point, he accidentally left evidence behind. Leopold recalled: "We gathered up all the clothes, placed them in the robe and apparently at this point the glasses fell from my pocket. I carried the robe . . . a distance of some 300 yards, and one of the socks apparently dropped from the bundle."[34]

The two then drove back in the direction of Chicago. They went to a drugstore to post the ransom letter the Franks would receive the following day, and Leopold called the Franks home to tell them Bobby had been kidnapped.

Police inspect the drainage pipe at Wolf Lake where Bobby Franks's body was found.

The two men then drove into their neighborhood. They stopped at Loeb's house where they burned Franks's clothes in the furnace. They did not burn the auto robe, however, because it was too big and would smell up the house. They also quickly cleaned the blood from the back seat and footwells of the car and drove it to Leopold's house where they left it on Greenwood Avenue amid other cars where it would not be noticed. That evening they socialized with Leopold's father until he went up to bed. After they were sure he was asleep, Leopold and Loeb left the house and disposed of the remaining evidence, throwing the chisel out and burning the auto robe.

A Plan Gone Awry

The next day, Thursday, Leopold and Loeb met again on campus at 11 A.M. after Leopold's classes. They had lunch with a friend and then went to Leopold's house where they cleaned the rental car more thoroughly with soap and brushes.

They drove the rental car to a train station at Twelfth Street where Loeb briefly boarded the 3 P.M. train to Michigan City. There, he left a letter of instruction in the telegraph car for Jacob Franks to find. Meanwhile, Leopold phoned Franks and gave him instructions to meet at the drugstore where they planned to call him and instruct him to board the Michigan City train, giving him no time to confer with police. From the letter on the train he would be instructed where to throw the bundle of money from the moving train, and Leopold and Loeb would be there to collect it.

As they drove to the drugstore to place the call, Loeb picked up a midday edition of the *Chicago Journal*. The headlines announced the discovery of a boy found near Wolf Lake. Leopold later recalled their reaction: "Absorbedly we read the story together. But there was no identification [of the body]. They didn't know who it was. Maybe we were still all right."[35]

They decided they had nothing to lose by attempting to finish their plan. They telephoned Franks and gave him instructions to go to a pay phone at the Van de Bogert and Ross drugstore. An hour later they telephoned the drugstore, unaware that Bobby Franks's body had been identified in the time since their previous call. Leopold dialed the drugstore and asked for Franks. Franks was not there. He waited a few minutes and then called again. Franks was still not there. The plan ended. "We gave it up as a bad job,"[36] Leopold said.

Neither Leopold nor Loeb believed that their crime would be traced back to them. However, it was only a week later that the trail of evidence they had left led police to them. Their confessions marked the end of the most publicized manhunt in the history of Chicago.

Chapter 4

An Airtight Case

WHILE THE CRIME against Bobby Franks and the murder investigation that followed had been a significant story in Chicago, after the announcement of Leopold and Loeb's confessions the story gained international attention. That Franks had been murdered by his wealthy, well-respected neighbors was big news. Papers in many parts of the world stated that the crime was the worst sort of murder. For instance the *New British Statesman*, a London newspaper, said, "The great Chicago murder case . . . stands alone in the records of crime. Sensational murders are common enough. . . . But no crime that the modern world knows of can be set beside the killing of the boy Robert Franks by Nathan Leopold and Richard Loeb."[37]

This level of interest by the media and the public who read about the crime created an atmosphere of anger and indignation. Many in the public called for a swift trial followed by execution, and, with the confessions and evidence the prosecution gathered, it seemed likely that the case would go this way. However, the families of the accused men hired Clarence Darrow—one of the nation's most renowned defense attorneys and a staunch opponent of the death penalty—to represent their sons. This action made it clear to prosecutors and the public that Leopold and Loeb, despite their confessions and the evidence against them, were not going to the gallows without a fight.

Hiring Darrow

Despite their initial disbelief that Leopold and Loeb's confessions could be true, their families recognized their need for a defense. Leopold's brother Mike and Loeb's uncle Jacob hired Benjamin C. Bachrach, a successful Chicago defense attorney. They also sought out the help of Clarence Darrow, a renowned civil rights attorney who lived nearby. Saturday night, Jacob Loeb arrived at the apartment of Clarence Darrow with the intent to hire him. Darrow's wife answered and told Loeb that her husband was sick in bed, but Loeb pushed past her and entered Darrow's bedroom where he pleaded with the attorney to defend his nephew and Leopold. He promised to pay any fee necessary to keep the men from hanging.

Darrow had heard of the case and understood the dire circumstance of the accused. He was ill, aged, and tired, but he saw in the case an opportunity to fight against his great foe, the death penalty. He later wrote: "I wanted to lend a hand, and I wanted to stay out of the case. . . . The public and press were almost

A MAN WITH A MISSION

Born into a poor but liberal and activist family in the rural community of Kinsman, Ohio, in 1857, Clarence Darrow studied law at the University of Michigan Law School and was admitted to the Ohio bar in 1878. He practiced as a country lawyer in numerous small towns in Ohio until he moved to Chicago in 1888 to practice as a corporate lawyer for the Chicago and North Western Railway.

During his career he was noted for his courtroom skills and his wide-ranging concern regarding injustice in society. He became a labor and criminal lawyer, reformer, and social critic.

In his later years he became widely known as a lecturer advocating progressive causes, taking on prohibition, prison reform, evolution, the relationship of science to society, and the death penalty. Leaving his job as a corporate attorney when he was thirty-seven years old, he turned to private practice as a defense attorney for nearly two thousand courtroom battles. Among his clients were murderers, Communists, Socialists, and activists.

During his career he successfully saved over 180 people from the death sentence. In his essay "The Loeb-Leopold Case," excerpted from Albert Halper's *The Chicago Crime Book*, Darrow wrote, "No client of mine had ever been put to death and I felt it would almost kill me if it should ever happen."

He would never have to find out. He died of natural causes in 1938 after sixty years of practicing law.

Defense attorney Clarence Darrow saved over 180 people from the death sentence, prior to taking on the Leopold and Loeb case.

solidly against me. In a terrible crisis there is only one element more helpless than the poor, and that is the rich . . . and I dreaded the fight. . . . But I went in, to do what I could.[38]

Leopold and Loeb Examined

The following day, Sunday, June 1, Darrow attempted to contact his clients. However, he was not permitted to do so. State's Attorney Crowe wanted to keep the young men away from counsel as long as he could so that he could obtain as much information as possible out of them before Darrow could tell them to stop talking.

That Sunday, in addition to completing the scavenger hunt for evidence with the defendants, Crowe had five psychologists—then known as "alienists"—interview the two accused men. Because of the confessions and seemingly insurmountable amount of evidence against the defendants, Crowe understood that the only defense possible for the case would have to be to enter a plea of not guilty by reason of insanity. Therefore, he hired the doctors to examine the defendants so that the psychiatrists could later testify to Leopold and Loeb's sanity.

In a strategic maneuver, Crowe had hired five of the city's foremost specialists in mental illness—doctors Hugh Patrick, Archibald Church, Harold Douglas Singer, William O. Krohn, and Rollin Turner Woodyatt—to testify for the prosecution. He moved quickly so that Darrow would not have the opportunity to hire them first. That afternoon, the doctors interviewed Leopold and Loeb and gave them thorough physical examinations.

Grand Jury Hearing and Arraignment

On Monday, June 2, Darrow and Bachrach appeared in court before Judge John R. Caverly, the criminal court chief justice who would later hear their case, to argue for their right to see their clients. Crowe argued against it, saying he needed a couple more days to complete his interrogation, but Caverly sided with the defense. Leopold and Loeb were transferred from Crowe's care to jail. The attorneys spoke to their new clients and, as expected, Darrow instructed the young men to stop providing evidence against themselves to the prosecutors and the press. Later that afternoon, Darrow allowed the men to speak to the press; however, to every question regarding the crime, Leopold and Loeb each declined to answer. "We cannot talk without advice of counsel,"[39] they said.

On Thursday, June 5, the grand jury of the criminal court of Cook County assembled to hear the case. After hearing seventy-one witnesses for three days, the court voted to indict Leopold and Loeb on eleven counts of murder and sixteen counts of kidnapping.

The following week, on June 11, Leopold and Loeb again appeared in the criminal court for their arraignment. That

THE RIGHT TO REMAIN SILENT

When Leopold and Loeb were arrested in May 1924, they were held without being charged until they confessed. Following their confessions, State's Attorney Crowe refused their attorneys access to them so that he could get as much information as possible.

In his book *Leopold and Loeb: Crime of the Century*, Hal Higdon quotes an exchange between Darrow and Crowe during the hearing in which Darrow accuses the prosecutor of violating his clients' civil rights in these actions. Crowe answers defiantly, "I will confess that I violated a number of constitutional rights and I intend to continue that as long as I am state's attorney. When a man is charged with a crime I am not going to telephone him and ask him to hire a lawyer before I talk to him." Darrow responds angrily: "Well I don't think in a well-organized, intelligent community, a man could be elected state's attorney under the statement that when a man is charged with the crime the state's attorney would violate his constitutional rights."

At the time, Crowe's actions were entirely legal as there was no law requiring police to inform persons under arrest of the right to have an attorney present during questioning. Years later, in 1966, in the *Miranda v. Arizona* case, the U.S. Supreme Court ruled that the accused must be read their rights prior to questioning. The warning, now called the Miranda warning, reads: "You have the right to remain silent. Anything you say can and will be used against you in a court of law.

You have the right to speak to an attorney, and to have an attorney present during any questioning. If you can not afford a lawyer, one will be provided for you at government expense."

morning, the courtroom doors opened to admit spectators. Bailiffs were stampeded by the public and the press, who mobbed the court in search of seats, hoping to catch a glimpse of the defendants. Leopold and Loeb sat calmly as their attorneys entered a not guilty plea.

Caverly set the court date for August 4, 1924, and set a deadline of July 21 for counsel to submit all pretrial motions such as a request for a delay in the trial date, a change of location for the trial, or a change in plea.

Building a Defense

Darrow, Bachrach, and the third attorney to join the defense, Bachrach's younger brother Walter, an attorney with an interest in psychology, began assembling a defense for their clients. They had just a little more than three weeks to do so.

Darrow and the Bachrachs' strategy was to keep their clients from the death penalty. However, with the full confessions, the evidence provided by Leopold and Loeb themselves, and the men's free and often damning comments to the press, the attorneys had a challenging task before them. Darrow recalled, "We knew that seldom had a case been handled like this one; and everyone, far and near, had made up their minds what should be done."[40] Darrow's first strategy was to have the defendants examined by psychiatrists with equal reputation to those hired by the prosecution. For this they hired five psychiatrists, among them the most prominent doctors in the country: William Alanson White, William Healy, and Bernard Glueck, who would serve as the primary expert witnesses; and Carl M. Bowman and Harold S. Hulbert, who would make an extensive psychiatric and physical examination of both men and write a report for use in court.

The physicians each conducted all-day interviews with Leopold and Loeb over the three-week period leading up to the trial. They also interviewed members of their families and spoke to their former governesses about the young men's childhoods.

Leopold enjoyed the interviews, liking the attention and the opportunity to talk about himself and display his keen intellect. In contrast, Loeb fell asleep out of boredom during many of the sessions. As Hal Higdon wrote, Leopold and Loeb's behavior during these interviews had a lasting impact on how they were perceived:

> The legend of Leopold and Loeb has been colored partly by the attitude each brought to his psychiatric examinations. Psychiatrists are supposed to be coolly objective scientists. But Darrow's alienists came away from their examinations totally enamored of Nathan Leopold, but disliking Richard Loeb.[41]

Surprise Maneuver

As the date of the trial grew near, the defense attorneys continued to build their case; however, Darrow realized that there was little likelihood that his clients would escape death if their fate was placed in the hands of a jury. Thus, he recommended that the defendants change their plea to guilty. He explained that

JAILBIRDS

During the weeks before their court appearance, when they were not being examined by psychiatrists, Leopold and Loeb were growing accustomed to life in jail. As Maureen McKernan wrote in her book *The Amazing Crime and Trial of Leopold and Loeb*, "before many days passed, one might have thought the boys had lived there forever." At first the two were treated as celebrities by other inmates who had heard about their case through the newspapers. Even after the special interest in them wore off, though, the two adapted surprisingly well, making friends with other inmates and participating in conversations and sports. Additionally, they enjoyed extra comfort and privileges that their families' money afforded them. For instance, they rarely ate the prison fare because their families had specially prepared dinners brought in from restaurants. Their neverending supply of cigarettes given to them by their families also helped them remain popular, as they were generous in distributing them among other inmates.

Although they were housed in separate cells and did not socialize much with each other, Leopold and Loeb had their first opportunity to speak alone in private one day in mid-July after Loeb had been moved to the same floor of the prison as Leopold. Maureen McKernan reports in her book *The Amazing Crime and Trial of Leopold and Loeb*, that Leopold approached Loeb with the offer to make amends and repair their friendship. "Dick, we've quarreled before, and made up, let's forget and start again," he said. Loeb agreed and shook hands, and the two prepared to face their fate together.

Jail inmates initially treated Leopold (left) and Loeb as celebrities.

with a plea of guilty there would be no jury trial, just a hearing before a judge. Although pleading guilty ensured that his clients would go to prison, Darrow felt he could more easily convince one judge to spare the lives of his clients than he could convince twelve jury members to do so.

Further, in an attempt to mitigate the punishment, he would ask that the court consider testimony from the psychiatrists and other witnesses, which he hoped would show that his clients' mental state contributed to their crime.

The defendants and their families agreed to the change in plea. On Monday, July 21, Darrow appeared before Caverly and surprised everyone in the courtroom with the announcement. He said:

> We believe [the defendants] should be permanently isolated from society. . . . As to the motions against these two . . . we can find no substantial thing to criticize. . . . After long reflection and thorough discussion . . . we have determined to make a motion to this court for each of the defendants . . . to withdraw our pleas of not guilty and enter pleas of guilty. . . . The statute [law] provides that evidence may be offered in mitigation of the punishment and we shall ask . . . that we may be permitted to offer evidence as to the mental condition of these young men to show the degree of responsibility they had and also to offer evidence as to the youth of these defendants and the fact of a plea of guilty as further mitigation of penalties in this case. With that we throw ourselves upon the mercy of this court.[42]

Pursuit of the Death Penalty

The change of plea offered by Darrow was a surprise to everyone in the courtroom except those behind the defense table. State's Attorney Crowe responded with hostility to the tactic, arguing that the prosecution would still present its case against the defendants in pursuit of the death penalty. He said:

> The fact that the two murderers have thrown themselves on the mercy of the court does not in any way

alleviate the enormity of the crime they have committed. . . . The State will present its entire case in the same
manner we would have presented it to a jury in the box.
. . . There is only one punishment which will satisfy the
prosecution. . . . They have thrown themselves upon the
mercy of the court and we will demand they be
hanged.[43]

Despite the prosecutor's objections, Caverly agreed to hear
the psychiatric evidence offered by the defense in mitigation of
the sentence. Caverly's decision to hear this evidence set an
important legal precedent since in the past such evidence had
never been used for this purpose. Previously, psychiatric evidence had been used exclusively to show that the defendant was
insane and not responsible for his or her actions, and therefore
not subject to punishment. However, for this strategy to work for
the defense, they had to prove that while the men were sane,
their degree of responsibility was in question due to their state
of mind, which Darrow hoped to prove was not normal. The difference was fine but legally important.

A Crowded Courtroom

After announcing his decision to hear the mitigating evidence,
Caverly moved the date of the hearing to July 23, only two days
later. On that morning, exactly nine weeks after their crime,
Leopold and Loeb appeared in court for the first day of the hearing that would decide their fates.

The change of the defendants' plea had even more greatly
increased press and public attention to the case, and although
the summer heat had soared and the courtroom was sweltering,
more than three thousand people requested seats in the three-
hundred-person-capacity courtroom.

The room was densely packed with the press, the public,
telegraph operators, relatives of the accused, bailiffs, and the
defendants themselves. Additionally, there were eight attorneys
present: The state was represented by Crowe, Thomas Marshall,
Joseph P. Savage, Milton Smith, and John Sbarbaro; the defense

Darrow (left), Loeb (second from right), Leopold (right), and others stand before Chief Justice Caverly during the pair's hearing in July 1924.

by Darrow and the two Bachrach brothers. Finally, Chief Justice Caverly appeared, the final person to enter the room.

Prosecution Opens Its Case

Crowe opened the prosecution's case that first day by saying the state planned to show the murder and kidnapping of Robert Franks to be the "most cruel, cowardly, dastardly murder ever committed in the annals of American jurisprudence."[44] He added that the defendants' guilt was so certain that there was no punishment other than the penalty of death suitable for the crimes.

Over the next week Crowe called numerous witnesses to the stand to prove his case against the defendants. The defense cross-examined almost none of them. As defense counsel repeatedly reminded the court, the defendants admitted their guilt, so there was no point in arguing the case. However, Crowe insisted.

Among the first witnesses were Jacob and Flora Franks. Mrs. Franks's appearance was described by reporters as one of the most powerful testimonies because of her distraught condition.

One reporter said that she was "a figure of listless sorrow, reticent in her grief, terrible in her voice, and hopelessly unmindful of the future."[45]

Other witnesses to testify for the prosecution that first day were Edwin Gresham, who had identified Franks's body; Joseph Springer, the coroner's physician, who testified to the cause of death and the condition of the body; and other forensic specialists who testified to the results of various tests performed on the body.

Over the next six days of testimony, Crowe brought forward a parade of witnesses, many of whom were questioned only for a few minutes. These included Leopold family servants, clerks who had sold the chisel and acid to the men, and the pharmacist who had received the call meant for Jacob Loeb the day after the kidnapping.

Bobby Franks's mother Flora was one of eighty-one witnesses to testify for the prosecution.

On July 24 Darrow rose in objection to the numerous witnesses being called to prove a crime to which the defendants had already pleaded guilty. "Your Honor, we object. . . . It is not necessary to question an unending line of witnesses to prove the thing that has been admitted. There is a plea of guilty here."[46] Crowe retorted, "A plea of guilty, yes, making a virtue of necessity. It was done because there was no escape. . . . We propose to pile up the evidence mountain so high there is no question but that these defendants get nothing less than their just desserts on the gallows."[47] Caverly overruled the objection, and Crowe continued to call witnesses.

Several witnesses were called to establish the motive of the crime as greed—that despite their wealth, Leopold and Loeb had committed the crime to get the ten thousand dollars in ransom. One witness called was Leon Mandel, a friend of Leopold's who testified that Leopold and Loeb played high-stakes bridge, often losing three to four hundred dollars a night, and thus possibly needed the money.

Other witnesses were called to show that the men knew the gravity of their crime. For instance, Leopold's professor of criminal law testified that several days after the murder Leopold had asked him to hypothetically discuss the Franks case. When the professor refused, Leopold persisted, saying that he believed that since the penalty for kidnapping was the same as that for murder, the law encouraged a kidnapper to kill his victim.

One witness, Detective Sergeant Gortland, was called to testify that Leopold had planned his guilty plea in advance. Gortland said that the day after Leopold and Loeb were arrested, "Leopold told me . . . 'If I plead guilty before a friendly judge I will get off with life imprisonment.'"[48] Gortland also told the court that Leopold said that he would have tried to kill himself rather than be arrested if he had known Loeb would confess. According to Gortland, Leopold said, "If I knew that Loeb was going to peach I could have killed myself and taken a couple of coppers with me."[49] Gortland added that he took Leopold seriously, as firearms had been found in his house—the same firearms the men had carried with them on their robbery of Loeb's former fraternity house in November 1923.

NO PITY FOR LEOPOLD

Following their confessions and throughout their sentencing hearing, Leopold and Loeb received enormous publicity from the press and spoke frequently with reporters. Leopold particularly enjoyed speaking to the media and was very concerned about what the public thought of him. As a July 27, 1924, *New York Times* story revealed, when one reporter indicated that people pitied him, Leopold said that he did not want anyone's pity:

> I do not want you to feel sorry for me, and if you do, I wish you would change your mind. I do not feel sorry for myself for what I did. I did it, that's all. I got myself in this jam, and it is up to me to get out. . . . I have great feeling for my father and my brothers, but not for myself. No! . . . Life is what we make it, and I appear to have made mine what it is today. That's my lookout and nobody else's.

Up to this point in the prosecution's presentation of its case Darrow had not cross-examined any witnesses, as the defense did not contest the facts of the crime. However, Leopold told Darrow that the detective was lying and insisted he cross-examine the witness. Darrow did so, asking Gortland to provide some documentation of this conversation. Gortland fumbled through his notes but was unable to find reference to the discussion. In fact, he was never able to locate his notes on this conversation although he insisted that the conversation occurred as he said it had. According to one reporter, Darrow got the last word by having Gortland restate that he had no written record of the alleged remark.

Prosecution Rests

The testimony for the prosecution ended on Wednesday, July 30, after eighty-one witnesses had testified. Although the defendants had admitted their guilt, there was little doubt that Crowe had proven the defendants' crimes thoroughly. Crowe hoped that the amount and seriousness of the evidence presented would convince Caverly to sentence the defendants to death. However, the defense had yet to present their case for mitigation. That afternoon, Clarence Darrow rose and called their first witness.

Chapter 5

Men of Diseased Minds

IN SUPPORT OF mitigation of Leopold and Loeb's sentence, Darrow intended to show that the defendants, although sane, were mentally diseased men. To prove this claim, the defense called on several renowned psychiatrists to give expert testimony as to the accused men's physical and mental abnormalities. The defense further hoped that such testimony would serve to humanize his clients in the eyes of the public and the court. However, the defense strategy faced immediate and repeated challenges from the prosecution.

A Legal Duel

The first challenge to the psychological testimony came on July 30, just as the first witness, William Alanson White, was called. White, along with several other psychologists, had examined the defendants while in the employ of defense counsel and their clients and intended to state his findings to the court.

Before the witness could begin, Crowe objected. He said it was apparent that the purpose of White's testimony was to prove the abnormal mental condition of the defendants at the time of the crime. Such evidence, he argued, was not allowed. He said:

> The law is conclusive on the point that an insane man cannot enter a plea of guilty. . . . If there is any attempt to raise the issue of insanity, I will insist that a jury be called at once. There is no such thing in the law as distinguishing whether

the man is 25 per cent or 30 per cent normal. He is either sane and responsible under the law or he is insane.[50]

Walter Bachrach argued that the defense made no claims of insanity. He said:

"Our plea of guilty in this case admits that on that day [of the crime] . . . they were legally sane; therefore we do not propose to offer any evidence to show that they were legally insane. We do propose to offer evidence, however, to show a mental condition, a mental disease."[51]

The Hulbert-Bowman Report

Crowe's objection to the admissibility of the defense's expert witness testimony may have also been influenced by the publication of a psychological report that had found its way into the press just days

Darrow meets with his clients outside court. Darrow's defense strategy was to prove that Leopold and Loeb were mentally diseased.

before White was called to the stand. Referred to as the Hulbert-Bowman report, it had been written by Harold S. Hulbert and Carl M. Bowman, psychiatrists employed by the defense team. The report was a several-thousand-page document based on several weeks of examinations of and interviews with Leopold and Loeb, as well as interviews with their families, servants, and friends.

The document discussed the defendants' family history, physical history, upbringing, academic history, sex life, fantasies, delinquencies, and psychological profiles. It drew the conclusion that there was a causal relationship between the biological makeup and upbringing of the two defendants and their delinquencies and mental states.

Hulbert and Bowman's report said that Loeb and particularly Leopold were physically abnormal and had experienced abnormal childhoods. Because of these factors, the psychiatrists argued, each defendant had suffered a split in their emotional and intellectual maturity: While the men were intelligent and accomplished, they were unable to experience normal emotional lives.

Insanity or Abnormality

Long excerpts from the report had been printed in many of the newspapers all over the country earlier in the week. After reading them, Crowe anticipated that the defense's expert witnesses would base their defense on the report's findings. Crowe objected to the testimony, saying that the defense was attempting to prove insanity without calling it insanity.

The debate continued for three days. Finally, on August 1 Caverly overruled Crowe's objection and agreed to hear the expert witness testimony of the doctors. The decision established a legal precedent allowing psychological evidence to be considered for mitigation of sentence, and as author Paula S. Fass writes, "The maneuver [by the defense] probably also cost Robert Crowe his public hanging."[52]

Expert Witness Testimony

On August 4 the defense brought their psychiatric team to the stand. From the start it was clear that Crowe's concerns were well-founded. Although the Hulbert-Bowman report was not allowed to be read to the court, their joint testimony reinforced the findings of the document.

The doctors' testimony began with a discussion of the defendants' physical and psychological history. The first subject addressed was Loeb's physical history, the main abnormalities of which were a delayed physical maturity and some nervous disorders.

Judge Caverly agreed to hear the defense's expert witness testimony. His decision to do so saved Leopold and Loeb from hanging.

The doctors said that from the age of four, Loeb had been raised by a governess named Emily Struthers, a twenty-eight-year-old Canadian to whom Loeb grew very close. Struthers read to Loeb frequently and helped him with his schoolwork. Because of her attention, Loeb was so well prepared for school by the time he began that he skipped several grades.

However positive her influence was, Struthers was also a strict disciplinarian who punished Loeb whenever he displeased her or violated one of her many rules. Because of this Loeb developed a habit of lying to escape punishment. He soon found it easy to hide or lie about the things he did that she did not like. He also began lying to others.

Loeb's Criminal Fascination

Although Struthers disapproved of it, Loeb also secretly developed a fascination with magazine crime stories, which he read obsessively. According to the defense psychiatrists, these stories had a profound influence on his psychological development. Around the age of ten or eleven he developed a vivid fantasy life about being a criminal. Eventually, the fantasies evolved into scenarios in which he was a master criminal, so clever at planning crimes that he could escape detection from the greatest detectives in the world.

The childish imaginings turned to antisocial behavior over a period of years as he began putting his fantasies into use. He planned burglaries of people's homes and indulged in petty thefts, frequently stealing money or items for the thrill of it.

Fantasies about kidnapping also figured into Loeb's early psychological development. Hulbert said: "In early childhood [Loeb] was strongly impressed by a story of kidnapping in a book which he had read and the crime of kidnapping seemed to him to be the maximum crime. . . . [T]here had been [in him a] growing . . . ambition to commit kidnapping and make it a perfect mysterious crime."[53] The psychiatrists said that although Loeb could be a pleasant young man, his criminal fantasies, combined with his increasingly frequent lying, developed into a serious emotional problem which caused his life to veer away from productive and healthy interests.

LIVING HIS FANTASY

According to Hal Higdon in his book *Leopold and Loeb: Crime of the Century*, as a result of Loeb and Leopold's crime and the proceedings which followed, Loeb's fantasy life of criminal celebrity was achieved. Higdon writes:

Fantasy became reality for Richard Loeb as a result of the celebrity he and his partner achieved by their crime. The two thrill killers, but particularly Loeb, fascinated young women who wept at their plight, used every ruse to gain entrance to the courtroom, and, once inside, often attempted to reach them or pass them notes. . . . Richard Loeb seemed to relish his celebrity in court. Jail for Loeb thus may have been more reward than punishment. He was finally living the life he had fantasized as a boy. He preferred to wear ragged clothes in his cell rather than the fine clothes his money could buy. "He felt comfortable in jail," suggested Dr. White, "felt as though he sort of belonged there."

Loeb's Other Emotional Abnormalities

Loeb's outward manner and appearance also hid several other emotional problems, including mood swings, depression, self-destructive impulses, and low self-esteem.

Loeb had experienced mood swings and depression since childhood. They were worst when he was alone, and the incidences had increased within the past two years. He also had considered suicide numerous times but had not gone through with it for one reason or another. White said, "All of Dickie's life has been in the direction of self-destruction."[54]

The doctors said that Loeb's self-destructive impulses were in part due to low self-esteem, which he hid behind an outward arrogance. They argued that his lying and antisocial behavior were also due in part to his desire to feel superior to others.

Finally, the doctors said that there was a dangerous split in Loeb's personality between his emotional and intellectual life that was responsible for much of his antisocial behavior. Dr. Glueck said: "This disorder is primarily in a profound pathological discord between his intellectual and emotional life. . . . This boy, while capable of orienting himself intellectually, is quite incapable of endowing these surroundings with an adequate emotion."[55]

Leopold's Childhood

Concurrently, the experts testified to Leopold's physical and mental condition. They hypothesized that Leopold's antisocial behavior had grown out of his physical abnormalities and his childhood experiences.

Leopold had been a weak and sickly child who suffered from several abnormalities and malfunctions in his endocrine glands. This, doctors said, had been responsible for his slight build and various physical deformities such as prominent eyes. They argued that these problems were also responsible for several of the positive and negative psychological attributes displayed in his childhood and early adulthood.

Some of these attributes were Leopold's early development, intelligence, and ease of learning. He had spoken his first words at four months and walked at fourteen months.

Like Loeb, Leopold was not raised by his mother. His mother was ill throughout Leopold's childhood, so he was raised by a series of governesses, the third and last of which was a significant influence on him. An Alsatian woman named Mathilda Wantz, she came to the Leopold household when Leopold was about six years old and remained until he was twelve. According to Leopold, Wantz took the place of his mother in many ways.

However, in interviews with Wantz and other members of the Leopold family, doctors discovered that she had been a strong negative influence on Leopold. Described in the Hulbert-Bowman report as "homely, suspicious, irritable, not tactful, jealous, over-sexual in unusual ways, scheming, and very immature in her judgement,"[56] Wantz had been sexually abusive and inappropriate with Leopold and his brother. She exposed herself to the boys, insisting that they closely inspect her naked body. She also fondled them during baths and miseducated them sexually. Further, she encouraged Leopold to do dishonest things such as stealing from another boy, and then blackmailed him with the crime, threatening to tell on him.

Wantz was eventually fired; however, the doctors contended that her negative influence outlasted her physical presence in Leopold's life. According to the Hulbert-Bowman report, "She gave [Leopold] a wrong original conception about sex, about theft, about right and wrong, about selfishness, about secrecy. He was so constituted that he was never able to emancipate himself from her erroneous teachings and mistakes."[57]

HISTORIC INSPIRATION

According to alienists for the defense, Loeb had been strongly affected as a young child by a story of a kidnapping that may have served as his inspiration for the Franks kidnapping and murder. The story was that of the kidnapping of Charley Ross, here detailed courtesy of the Independence Hall Association website (www.ushistory.org):

On July 1, 1874 two little boys were abducted in front of their family's mansion. It was the first kidnapping for ransom in the history of the United States. . . .

The boys were named Charley and Walter Ross; they were 4 and 6 years old. The two men who kidnapped them had given the boys candy on previous occasions. That day, however, the men told the boys to climb into their buggy and promised to buy them firecrackers. The boys boarded and they drove off into the city. Charley would never be seen again.

As they drove farther away, Charley wanted to go home and began to cry. The men stopped in front of a store and gave Walter 25 cents. He entered the store and started choosing firecrackers, while the men drove away with Charley.

The boys' father, Christian K. Ross, thought the boys were playing in a neighbor's yard. But soon a neighbor told him that she saw the boys traveling in a buggy. The father began the search for his son that he would continue until his death in 1897. He didn't tell his wife at first, who was recovering from an illness in Atlantic City. Two days later, however, she found out when he began advertising in the newspapers for his sons' return. A stranger found Walter and returned him to his father. Walter related the tale.

Two days after that, the father received a crude note, saying that Charley would be released for a sum of money. On July 7, came another note demanding $20,000 and instructing the boy's father how to go about paying the kidnappers. The father tried to follow the instructions as best he could but never contacted the kidnappers.

Expert witnesses for the defense testified that Leopold (right) and Loeb's childhood experiences were responsible for their pathological behavior.

Leopold's Personality

Doctors testified that Wantz had unhealthily influenced Leopold's perception of himself, as had his wealth and advanced abilities. His early academic accomplishments, his high IQ, and his ability to learn quickly encouraged Leopold to believe that he was a superior being, set apart from others and not subject to the rules and morals of other lesser people. He believed whatever gave him pleasure was right. This delusion was so extreme, according to the doctors, that "even the commission of murder is perfectly tolerable to him on this basis of his conception of himself,"[58] they said.

Leopold also exhibited an abnormal lack of emotion in his personality. Since childhood, he had been suspicious of emotion and sentiment and had purposefully trained himself to be free of these qualities. Because of this, as in Loeb, doctors found in Leopold a split in his intellectual and emotional development. Dr. Healy noted that Leopold's lack of emotion was particularly cold-blooded: "Leopold told me that he could contemplate committing a murder with no more conscience than was necessary in selecting the sort of pie for dinner."[59]

Leopold's Self-Perception and Fantasy Life

According to the doctors, Leopold's antisocial personality was also rooted in his physical abnormalities, which made him nonatheletic and unable to participate in normal outdoor activities with his peers. This inferiority encouraged him to indulge in a fantasy life in which his desire for physical strength and ability could be satisfied.

Leopold's fantasies began when he was five years old. His most powerful fantasies involved his being a slave to a king. He envisioned himself as very good-looking and as the strongest

LEOPOLD'S MOTIVE

In cross-examining each of the expert witnesses for the defense, Crowe pressed the doctors to provide the motive for the murder. None could provide one beyond what the men had said: that they had intended it as an exercise, as a means of having some fun in the plotting and execution. Later, in his memoir, *Life Plus 99 Years*, Leopold wrote that he did not know why they did it:

> What was the motive for the crime? That sounds like a simple, straightforward, unambiguous question. It isn't. It contains the tacit assumption, for one thing, that my motive was the same as Dick's—that we were acting, in a sense, as one person. Nothing could be farther from the truth.
> My motive . . . was to please Dick. Just that—incredible as it sounds. I thought so much of the guy that I was willing to do anything—even commit murder—if he wanted it bad enough. And he wanted to do this—very badly indeed.

man in the world, and in the fantasies he would fight to defend his king against great odds.

As Leopold grew older, that fantasy persisted and he began seeking out real-life men with whom he could live out the king/slave scenarios. The doctors concluded that Loepold became so unhealthily obsessed with this desire that he had trouble distinguishing between the actualities of the real and his fantasies. This difficulty grew worse when he met Loeb, whom Leopold saw as a superior man to be revered and loved.

A Secret Compact

It was when Leopold and Loeb met, according to the doctors, that the serious trouble in their lives began. Each had psychological problems before they met, but it was the combination of their two personalities that made possible the crime against Bobby Franks. Dr. Glueck said: "I think the Franks crime was perhaps the inevitable outcome of this curious coming together of two pathologically disordered personalities, each one of whom brought into the relationship a phase of their personality which made their contemplation and the execution of the crime possible."[60]

While most of the public was by this time familiar with the criminal history of Leopold and Loeb, the testimony given at the hearing brought out facts about the sexual nature of Leopold and Loeb's relationship that had been only suspected or hinted at before. The Hulbert-Bowman report contained this information; however, the portions of the report discussing this part of the men's relationship were never printed in the newspapers because of concerns of indecency. During this portion of the hearing, testimony regarding the men's sexual activities together was spoken only to the judge and counsel at the bench so that the public, including reporters, could not hear it.

According to the doctors' testimony, Leopold and Loeb's criminal and sexual relationship were intertwined. Early in their friendship, Leopold had sexually propositioned Loeb and been refused. However, Loeb later agreed to Leopold's homosexual desires on the condition that Leopold would commit crimes with him. This secret compact set in motion the criminal activity that was to follow, culminating with their so-called perfect crime of kidnapping and murdering Bobby Franks.

Other Witnesses

Expert witness testimony for the defense concluded on Thursday, August 7. Afterward, defense counsel called several friends and associates of Leopold and Loeb to support the clinical evidence.

Darrow intended to call both Leopold's and Loeb's girlfriends, Lorraine Nathan and Germaine Reinhardt. Nathan was called to the stand and spoke of her former sweetheart Loeb with tears in her eyes. She testified that in the days before his arrest, Loeb's personality had changed. He had become "irrational, irresponsible, and infantile."[61] Under cross-examination, Crowe badgered Nathan relentlessly and even accused her of perjuring to help Loeb. Following her testimony, newspaper reporters swarmed around her asking questions and taking photographs as she left the courtroom. Disgusted with her treatment by the prosecution and the press, Darrow decided not to subject Leopold's girlfriend, Reinhardt, to the same treatment and did not call her after all.

On Tuesday, August 12, Darrow called his last witnesses, Loeb's father's secretary and Leopold's brother Mike Leopold, who testified that both of the defendants were so well provided for financially that the motive for their crime could not have been the ransom money. Albert Loeb's secretary stated Loeb received frequent checks for sizable sums whenever he wanted; meanwhile, Mike Leopold said that his brother received an allowance of $125 a month, which was more than most adult men made. Further, Leopold had been promised three thousand dollars spending money for a trip to Europe that summer.

With that testimony concluded, the defense rested its case. With their ten days of defense testimony, Darrow and his associates hoped that they had changed the public and court's perception of the defendants.

Judge Caverly addresses the court during the sensational trial.

Rebuttal

Although the prosecution had rested its case, Crowe presented more witnesses in rebuttal following the defense's presentation of its witnesses. He was unhappy with the defense's expert witness testimony and now brought forward numerous witnesses, including his own psychiatric team, to testify to the mental condition of the defendants. In the days of testimony that followed, Crowe called doctors Partick, Church, Singer, Krohn, and Woodyatt, each of whom had examined the defendants the day after they had delivered their confessions and prior to being allowed to see their attorney.

On the stand, the doctors dismissed the testimony of the defense expert witnesses, claiming that they had found no evidence of mental disease in the defendants during their examinations. They said that each defendant had been rational, possessed good memory, was of excellent intellectual ability, and showed apparent good judgment. Patrick summed up the psychiatric team's appraisal. He said: "Unless we assume that every man who commits a deliberate, cold-blooded, planned murder must, by the fact, be mentally diseased, there is no evidence of mental disease."[62]

After a week of rebuttal testimony, Crowe believed he had introduced sufficient doubt regarding the defense's argument for mental disease. On the afternoon of Tuesday, August 19, the prosecution rested again.

With the testimony for both sides complete, the stage was set for the most anticipated portion of the trial, the summary arguments. In these speeches, the prosecution and defense attorneys would make their final attempts to persuade Caverly to sentence the defendants according to their wishes.

Chapter 6

Showdown and Decision

THE FINAL DAYS of the Leopold Loeb hearing were among the most dramatic as the prosecution and defense attorneys presented their final arguments to the court. The addresses given by both sides were impassioned and emotional, and Darrow's in particular was so poignant that many in the court were deeply affected. As historian Douglas O. Linder wrote, "Few trial transcripts are as likely to bring tears to the eyes."[63]

Additionally, following final arguments, the drama of the trial built to a suspenseful climax as the defendants and the public anxiously waited two weeks for Judge Caverly's decision. Despite the varying speculation about the verdict, Caverly's decision surprised everyone.

Opening Speeches

The first addresses to the court were delivered by Assistant State's Attorneys Thomas Marshall and Joseph P. Savage. Each of the attorneys claimed that the murder of Bobby Franks was the most heinous crime that had ever been tried in the court, and they emphasized the duty of the court to assign what they claimed was the only suitable punishment: the death penalty.

Marshall said that no matter what the defense had tried to prove regarding mental disease, in the eyes of the law a person was either fully responsible for his or her behavior or not at all responsible. Thus, if Leopold and Loeb were not insane, as the defense had contended, then they were fully responsible for their actions and should receive the maximum penalty. He said, "If Leopold and Loeb are responsible enough to receive a sentence to the penitentiary, they are responsible enough for the extreme penalty."[64]

Savage emphasized the importance of the court's decision on this case, claiming that the fate of the death penalty depended on how these defendants were sentenced. He said:

[I]f your Honor does not hang both these murderers, it will be a long time in Cook County before we will hang another. Capital punishment will mean nothing in our law and might as well be abolished. . . . [T]he men who have reached the gallows prior to this time have been unjustly treated, if these two do not follow.[65]

Richard Loeb (left) and Nathan Leopold Jr. and the public waited two weeks for Judge Caverly's decision.

Educating the Court

Following the opening statements by the assistant state's attorneys, Walter Bachrach rose to speak first for the defense. Bachrach attempted to educate the court on mental disease and its significance to the case. Mental disease, he explained, was the inability to adjust to one's environment. One who suffers from mental disease is like a child who has not yet been socialized to the laws, rules, and morals of the world and thus cannot be held responsible for his or her actions. He presented several exhibits, including correspondence between the defendants, to support his argument that the young men suffered from mental disease. He also cited long passages from several psychiatric texts, including those written by doctors on the prosecution team, which indicated that Leopold had shown numerous signs of being paranoid and Loeb of being schizophrenic.

Bachrach also attacked the testimony by the psychiatrists for the prosecution who had denied such mental disease in the defendants. He claimed that the doctors had insufficiently examined the defendants. He said that the psychiatrists had claimed the defendants were mentally sound on the grounds that they showed outward signs of intelligence and awareness and that such conclusions were too simplistic. He said:

> To suppose that people are well mentally because they are well oriented to time, space and persons, because they know who they are and where they are, recognize people about them, show good memory, are logical and coherent in their responses to questions asked, is just as naive as to suppose that a person is mentally well because he is not a raving maniac.[66]

Darrow Speaks

The next day the most anticipated address, that of Clarence Darrow, began. In the last week of the hearing, public interest had waned and the crowds in the courtroom had thinned considerably. However, when it was announced in the press that Darrow would make his address on Friday, August 22, the crowds came in record numbers. Despite the ninety-seven degree heat in the unair-conditioned courtroom, the venue quickly filled beyond its capacity, and people packed into the halls and corridors outside. The noise from the crowd outside the courtroom door was so loud that when Darrow rose to deliver his argument on Friday morning, he had to stop twice, unable to be heard over the din. Finally, Caverly ordered the bailiffs to clear the floor outside the courtroom.

Darrow planned his speech to be the last of his career due to his age and failing health. He saw this as his last chance to fight against the death penalty in open court, so he had prepared a lengthy, elaborate speech embroidered with literary references, pathos, and emotion. Taking twelve hours over nearly three full days to deliver to the court, the speech is considered by many a masterpiece of legal oratory.

Although the address was nearly thirty-five thousand words long and reiterated many of the points made over the days of testimony for the defense, there were four central themes to which Darrow repeatedly returned in his speech:

1. Despite their precocious intellectual abilities, the defendants were children (in 1924, one was considered legally a child until the age of 21) with emotionally immature decision-making abilities.

2. The defendants were mentally diseased and thus not fully responsible for their actions.

3. There was no precedence in recent years in which defendants as young as Leopold and Loeb had been assigned the death penalty after pleading guilty.

4. The death penalty was a barbaric punishment not befitting a modern, enlightened age.

Renowned Harvard Law School professor and scholar Alan Dershowitz said that the speech is a masterpiece because of the clear logic of its arguments: "It's brilliance lies in the obviousness of

Clarence Darrow (right, standing) prepared his closing argument to be the last public condemnation of the death penalty of his career.

his arguments. He makes it easy for the listener to agree with him. He appeals to common sense, to every experience and to moral consensus. . . . [Y]ou begin to nod your head in agreement with his premises. Before long, he has you agreeing with his conclusions."[67]

Prejudice

Darrow began his address by acknowledging the unprecedented attention the case had received. He said that the relentless press coverage and the avid public interest had been one of the defense's greatest challenges because of the public's conception of justice. He said:

> Our anxiety over this case has not been due to the facts . . . but to the almost unheard-of publicity it has received. . . . [D]ay after day the people of Chicago have been regaled with stories of all sorts about it, until almost every person has formed an opinion. . . . And when the public is interested and demands a

punishment . . . great or small, it only thinks of one punishment, and that is death.[68]

Darrow argued that the press and public interest in the case was due to his clients' wealth, which had not only prejudiced the public against the defendants but had also motivated the prosecution to so relentlessly seek the death penalty. He said:

> I insist, Your Honor, that had this been the case of two boys of these defendants' ages, unconnected with families supposed to have great wealth, there is not a state's attorney in Illinois who would not have consented at once to a plea of guilty and a punishment in the penitentiary for life. Not one. . . . We are here with the lives of two boys imperiled, with the public aroused. For what? Because, unfortunately, the parents have money.[69]

Against the "Cry for Blood"

Darrow further revealed that in the entire history of the city, there had been 450 executions, only one of which had been carried out on defendants who pleaded guilty—and that man had been forty years old. However, he noted, the prosecution was almost delighted at the idea of executing his clients.

During their opening arguments, prosecutors Marshall and Savage had cited numerous precedents, many of them from the distant past, in which the death penalty had been assigned to youths. Darrow now turned to them and accused them of being bloodthirsty and primitive. He said:

> Lawyers stand here by the day and read cases from the Dark Ages, where judges have said that . . . a child if he was barely out of his cradle, could be hanged because he knew the difference between right and wrong. . . . I have heard in the last six weeks nothing but the cry for blood. . . . I have seen a court urged almost to the point of threats to hang two boys, in the face . . . of all the better and more humane thought of the age.[70]

THE ABCD CRIMES

After their confessions to the Franks murder, numerous Chicago newspapers speculated as to whether Leopold and Loeb had committed other unattributed crimes. During his interviews with Doctors Hulbert and Bowman, Loeb alluded to four other incidents, which the psychiatrists referred to as A, B, C, D. However, the doctors felt it was inadvisable to pursue this line of questioning, and when they did inquire further, they were told by both Leopold and Loeb that they refused to answer on advice of counsel. Nonetheless, in the September 1, 1924, issue of the *Chicago Tribune*, a front-page story speculated that Leopold and Loeb might have been responsible for the following four unsolved crimes:

A. The murder on November 25, 1923, of Freeman Louis Tracy, a part-time University of Chicago student whose body was thrown from an automobile. . . . He had been either kidnapped or lured into a[n automobile] while returning from a dance. There was evidence of a struggle which ended when a bullet smashed into Tracy's head.

B. The kidnapping and subsequent mutilation of Charles Ream, a taxi driver. Several hours after being dragged into an automobile and slugged on the morning of November 20, 1923, he regained consciousness on a deserted section of prairie on the far South Side. It is held significant that Ream positively identified Loeb and Leopold, following the latter's arrest for the Franks murder, as the youths responsible. . . .

C. The murder of Melvin T. Wolf, a young man who lived . . . a few blocks north of the Franks and Loeb residences. . . . [H]e set out to mail a letter . . . [and] no trace was found until his body was taken from [a] lake. . . .

D. The murder about two years ago of the "Handless Stranger." The nude body of this man, never identified, was found in the snow near Geneva. His hands had been hacked off.

Over time, other speculations arose about Leopold and Loeb's possible involvement in additional crimes, including a series of murders in which a chisel was used. However, there was never sufficient evidence to prosecute Leopold and Loeb for any of these crimes. The ABCD riddle remains unsolved.

A Senseless, Motiveless Crime

Darrow then set out to show the mentally diseased condition of his clients. Aware that the judge had heard esteemed psychiatrists for the prosecution deny the claim, he argued that even without the testimony of his own psychiatric team, it was apparent that his clients were not normal by the senselessness of their crime. He said:

> Here were two boys with good intellect, one eighteen and one nineteen. They had all the prospects that life could hold out for any of the young. . . . And they gave it all up for nothing. . . . They did not reason; they could not reason; they committed the most foolish, most unprovoked, . . . most causeless act that any two boys ever committed . . . not for money; not for spite; not for hate. They killed him as they might kill a spider or a fly, for the experience. They killed because they were made that way. Because somewhere in the infinite processes that go to the making up of the boy or the man something slipped.[71]

Darrow emphasized how risky and inept their so-called perfect crime had been. They had kidnapped and murdered Franks in broad daylight on a busy street, carried the body with them in the car for hours, and left a trail of evidence behind that had led police to them within ten days of the act. "I do not believe that there is any man who knows this case," he said, "who does not know that it can be accounted for only on the theory of the mental disease of these two lads."[72]

Darrow admitted that there was no simple explanation for why the crime happened or why the defendants had become the people who they were. He suggested that any number of influences could have corrupted these young men, from hereditary factors to environmental factors. Whatever the causes, however, Darrow maintained that they were not the fault of his clients and thus they were not responsible for their crimes and should not be punished with death. He said: "I am trying to say to this court that these boys are not responsible for this; and that their act was due to this and this, and this and this; and asking the court not to visit judgment of its wrath upon them for things for which they are not to blame."[73]

In his closing argument, Darrow maintained that Leopold and Loeb were mentally diseased and that they should not be punished with death.

Against Death

Finally, Darrow argued against the death penalty itself. He gave a summary history of the brutality of its use and argued that civilization had progressed beyond the use of such a barbaric solution to problems. He said:

> You can trace it all through the history of man. You can trace the burnings, the boilings, the drawings and quarterings, the hanging of people at the crossroads, carving

them up and hanging them as example for all to see. . . .
Gradually the laws have been changed and modified,
and men look back with horror at the hangings and the
killings of the past. . . . Do I need to argue to your Honor
that cruelty only breeds cruelty?—that hatred only
causes hatred?—that if there is any way to soften this
human heart . . . it is through charity, and love and understanding?[74]

Darrow concluded by pleading with the court not to return
to the dark past, not to, he said, "turn our faces backward to the
barbarism which once plagued the world."[75]

When he concluded, many in the court were weeping. Even
Caverly sat behind the bench with tears streaming down his
face. However, there was at least one man in the courtroom not
thus affected by the speech.

State's Attorney Crowe stood, dry-eyed and full of anger, to
deliver his own final plea.

A Frenzied Appeal

Crowe's speech was delivered with intense emotion and anima-
tion. Crowe's strategy seemed to be one of attack. He attacked
Darrow, calling him a protector of murderers, he attacked the
expert witnesses for presenting Leopold and Loeb as misguided
little boys when they were actually cold-blooded killers; but
most of all, he attacked Leopold and Loeb, referring to them as
"perverts . . . atheists . . . [and] murderers"[76]

Of his impassioned and frenzied speech, one reporter wrote:

Crowe gave the courtroom a mad day of it. He spoke in
a frenzy. He shouted and stamped and waved his arms.
Now he thrust his face, purple with strain of his apoplec-
tic speech, into the faces of Loeb and Leopold; now he
strode before Judge Caverly, shaking his fist as he put all
his lung power into some climax or another. It was all climax for that matter. . . . Into the faces of the two young
defendants he hurled epithet after epithet, his eyes blaz-
ing and his voice screaming anger.[77]

Point by Point

Point by point, Crowe argued against the defense's case. While Darrow had appealed to Caverly's humanity, Crowe assailed his sense of duty. He said that as people he and Caverly had the right to forgive Leopold and Loeb, but as public servants they could not. He said:

> I have a right to forgive those who trespass against me as I do, in the hopes that I in the hereafter will be forgiven my trespasses. As a private citizen I have that right, and as a private citizen I live that religion. But, as a public official . . . I have no right to forgive those who violate their country's laws. . . . Your honor has no right to forgive those who trespass against the State of Illinois.[78]

A DUBIOUS HONOR

Judge John Caverly was born in London in 1861 and emigrated to America with his family when he was six years old. His first job was as a waterboy in the steel mills of Chicago, and in his spare time he studied and attended night school. He eventually received his law degree at the age of thirty-six and was immediately given a position in the city attorney's office where he worked for five years before becoming elected a police magistrate.

In 1906 Caverly became the city attorney, during which time he cracked down on con artists and extortionists. After a four-year term, he was made a judge. He served on the bench for over twenty-five years, but by far his most famous case was the Leopold and Loeb hearing. Many, including Caverly himself, considered it a dubious honor at best. The fates of the defendants rested entirely on his decision and the public pressure was intense. He lost sleep many nights, and throughout the hearing he received thousands of letters, most of them urging him to hang the men, many threatening him with violence if he did otherwise. The threat grew to the point that he attended court under heavily armed guards on September 10, 1924, to deliver his decision to the court.

Following the hearing, it was stated that Caverly had been virtually a physical wreck from the case and his health was never entirely the same after the trial. Immediately after the sentencing he retired to hospital for treatment and a long rest. Soon after returning to the court, he transferred from the criminal to the civil court. He died fifteen years later, in August 1939, at age seventy-eight.

Crowe's speech then addressed every point of the defense's tactics and arguments. He argued against the contention that the defendants were men of diseased minds, going point by point through the Hulbert-Bowman report and testimony of the defense witnesses, attempting to find faults in the reasoning.

Crowe then turned to the defendants' ages as a defense against the death penalty. He argued that it was irrelevant. He said:

[I]f we can take the power of American manhood, take boys at eighteen years of age and send them to their death in the front line of trenches in France in defense of our laws, we have an equal right to take men nineteen years of age and take their lives for violating those laws that these boys gave their lives to defend.[79]

Finally, in his closing remarks Crowe returned to the testimony of one of his key witnesses, Sergeant Gortland, who had made the claim that Leopold had hoped to get off with a life sentence before a friendly judge. Crowe said:

I don't know whether your honor believes that officer or not, but I want to tell you, if you have observed these two defendants during the trial, if you have observed the conduct of their attorneys and their families . . . everybody connected with the case have laughed and sneered and jeered, and if the defendant, Leopold, did not say that he would plead guilty before a friendly judge, his actions demonstrated that he thinks he has got one.[80]

It was a misstep by the prosecutor because Caverly was angered by the remark and ordered it stricken from the record. Over the course of the hearing, Caverly had received hundreds of letters, many of them threatening him with violence if he did not sentence the defendants to death. Thus, he took Crowe's insinuating comment quite seriously. He said:

[The comment] could not be used for any purpose except to incite a mob and to try to intimidate this court. . . . The

PSYCHOLOGY AND THE LAW

Days before Judge Caverly's highly anticipated September 10, 1924, sentencing of Leopold and Loeb, George W. Kirchwey, a prison reformer whose background included being a former dean of the Columbia Law School and a former warden of Sing Sing Prison, wrote an article published in the September 7, 1924, edition of the *New York Times*. In it he wrote that he anticipated the impact of psychology on the law to be a profound and lasting improvement on the criminal justice system:

> I have known many criminals. Some of them were insane, some feeble-minded, some obviously psychopathic. But most of them have been so like our average humanity that I could not but marvel at the chance that had made criminals of them. In spite of the implications of the Leopold-Loeb case the citadel of the criminal law still stands four-square on its old foundations. It will not be shaken by the discovery that there are more shades and degrees of criminal responsibility than are written in its ancient records. . . . This is the way of the law. The more it changes, the more it stays the same.
>
> That does not mean, however, that the operation of criminal law will not be more closely approximate to justice in response to the developments such as Judge Caverly's hearing. The psychiatrist with his revolutionary science of human nature has come to stay. He will help the court identify the psychopathic personalities among the criminals awaiting trial or final disposition of their cases and will take them over for custodial care and treatment in institutions the State will provide for that purpose. . . .
>
> Whatever Judge Caverly's decision next Wednesday may be, the Leopold-Loeb case will go down in the annals of criminal procedure as a triumph for modern ideas of justice enlightened by the science of human psychology. That it should have received such unprecedented publicity will make its influence on criminal jurisprudence so much more profound. . . . [N]o one has failed to be impressed by the proceedings in Judge Caverly's courtroom.

State's Attorney knew that would be heralded all through this country and all over this world, and he knows the court hasn't an opportunity except to do what he did. . . . This court will not be intimidated by anybody at any time or place so long as he occupies this position.[81]

Although Crowe apologized, Caverly's anger remained and Crowe's speech ended poorly with the prosecution. In fact, many who have studied the case believe that the remark may have cost Crowe his victory.

After thirty-two days of testimony and arguments, the hearing of Leopold and Loeb came to an end. Caverly announced that he would deliver his decision in two weeks, on the morning of September 10. Court was adjourned.

Decision

On September 10 Caverly's courtroom was again crowded to capacity as the judge entered to deliver his decision. Everyone sat in quiet anticipation while he spoke at length before pronouncing sentence.

His first comments were disheartening to the defense counsel and particularly to the defendants. He said that the defendants'

Loeb, Darrow, and Leopold (left to right) listen as Judge Caverly pronounces a sentence of life imprisonment.

plea of guilty did not require that he handle the sentencing differently than a plea of not guilty. He further said that although he believed the young men were abnormal, he had not heard in the testimony of defense witnesses or comments of counsel any reason for mitigation.

He discussed the court's responsibilities for sentencing. He read aloud the requirements of sentencing under a plea of guilty for murder and for kidnapping, both of which were punishable by up to life imprisonment or death. He further stated that the law indicated no rule or policy for the guidance of his discretion in deciding sentence. However, he continued, because of the defendant's ages, he believed that a sentence of life imprisonment was harsh enough punishment. He said: "Life imprisonment, at the moment, strikes the public imagination as forcibly as would death by hanging, but to the offenders, particularly of the type they are, the prolonged suffering of years of confinement may well be the severest form of retribution and expiation."[82] He then sentenced Leopold and Loeb each to one sentence of life imprisonment for murder and one of ninety-nine years for kidnapping. Caverly brought down his gavel, making the sentence final and ending the most widely publicized and infamous criminal case in the history of the United States up to that time.

Epilogue

Aftermath

REACTION TO JUDGE Caverly's ruling in the Leopold and Loeb hearing was mixed. Clarence Darrow was pleased with the verdict, seeing it as a heartening victory against the death penalty. However, he recognized that it was not a blessing for his clients who faced life behind bars. He said: "Perhaps the sentence is worse than a death penalty for the two boys, but not for their families."[83]

Crowe responded to his defeat diplomatically. He said: "The state's attorney's duty was performed. . . . I don't intend, and have no desire, to criticize the decision of the court, but I still believe the death penalty is the only penalty feared by murderers."[84] Even the victim's father, Jacob Franks, responded well to the verdict, claiming that neither he nor his wife thought the defendants should be executed.

Many in the press were less forgiving. A reporter for the *New York Evening Sun* alleged that the defendants' wealth had purchased justice: "The sentence shakes the faith of the people in the blind equality of justice. They will not believe that any poor man who committed the crime . . . would have escaped death."[85] However, a reporter for the *New York Times* believed that Caverly's verdict had been based on the defendants' youth, not wealth:

> Judge Caverly bases his decision chiefly on the fact that the murderers are not of full age . . . concluding that the sparing of life under such circumstances appears to be the policy of the law, as well as in line with humane principles. . . . What the lawyers did or said for the defense

went for nothing. Judge Caverly simply ignored it. Had the youthful murderers been poor or friendless [rather than wealthy and respected], they would have escaped capital punishment precisely as Leopold and Loeb have escaped it.[86]

Leopold's own reaction was similar. He later wrote, "If Judge Caverly meant literally what he said in his opinion . . . the only thing that influenced him to choose imprisonment instead of death was our youth; we need only have introduced our birth certificates as evidence!"[87]

Adapting

While they felt fortunate to have escaped execution for whatever reason, Leopold and Loeb did not look forward to the fate that awaited them as they were taken the following day, September 11, 1924, to the Illinois State Penitentiary for Men, a maximum security prison nicknamed "Joliet" for its hometown of Joliet, Illinois. A photograph of the two taken shortly after their arrival at Joliet shows Leopold and Loeb—who had remained jovial and calm throughout most of their hearing—appearing uncharacteristically solemn and nervous.

Leopold and Loeb became prisoners 9306-D and 9305-D respectively, and their first years behind bars were difficult. They suffered illnesses and were kept away from each other. Loeb was transferred to another prison called Stateville, while Leopold remained at Joliet for several years, during which he was sent to solitary confinement several times, once for raising pigeons in his cell, another for allegedly assisting in a prison escape.

Together and Apart

However, their wealth provided some relief from prison life. Their families sent cash to them regularly, which kept them and their fellow inmates in cigarettes and other luxuries. Both eventually adjusted to their new surroundings. After several years of being apart, Leopold got himself transferred to Stateville Prison where he and Loeb again took up their friendship. The two

Leopold and Loeb were taken to Illinois State Penitentiary for Men (pictured), where they spent their first years behind bars together.

became model prisoners, using their education to open a correspondence school for other inmates, and Leopold used his talent for classification to reorganize the prison library. In between, they talked and played cards or handball.

However, the good times ended for the pair on January 28, 1936, when Loeb was attacked with a razor by inmate James Day, his cellmate. Later claiming Loeb had attempted to sexually attack him, Day had slashed Loeb from fifty-six to fifty-eight times. Leopold rushed to the surgery where his friend lay bleeding to death while doctors tried to save his life. Leopold was by his side when Loeb died.

Day was tried and acquitted for murder, the court believing his story about being attacked by Loeb. However, many, including Leopold, denied Day's story, indicating that the reason for the murder had been Loeb's inability to continue to supply Day with cigarettes and other items after the warden placed restrictions on the amount of money each prisoner could spend at the commissary.

Over the years following Loeb's death, Leopold became solitary and lonely. However, he also became a model prisoner. He took up his studies again, picking up twelve additional languages, learning calculus, hieroglyphics, and pursuing literature courses. Additionally, he continued to run the correspondence school he had started with Loeb, became an X-ray technician, and assisted in numerous studies of prison life.

Freedom

Leopold's behavior and accomplishments in prison were such that he was able to obtain release from prison in March 1958,

POPULAR CULTURE REMEMBERS
LEOPOLD AND LOEB

The kidnapping and murder of Robert Franks and the subsequent investigation and hearing made Leopold and Loeb the first celebrity murderers of twentieth-century America and has since inspired several fictionalized retellings:

Compulsion, a novel by Meyer Levin published in 1956 by Simon & Schuster, is based on the Leopold-Loeb case and became an immediate best seller. Leopold was unhappy with the novel and unsuccessfully sued Levin and the publishers after his release from prison.

The 1959 film version of the novel *Compulsion* stars Bradford Dillman and Dean Stockwell as Artie Strauss and Judd Steiner, the Loeb and Leopold characters, and Orson Welles as Jonathan Wilk, the Clarence Darrow character.

Alfred Hitchcock's 1948 classic movie thriller, *Rope*, based on the Patrick Hamilton play by the same name, features two gay New York college students who murder a friend for kicks.

Swoon, the 1991 film by Tom Kalin, a sexually frank retelling of the Leopold-Loeb case, focuses on the characters' homosexual relationship.

Never the Sinner, a play by John Logan first produced in 2001, is based on the crime and case.

Murder by Numbers, the 2003 film by Barbet Schroeder, was inspired by the Leopold-Loeb case and features two high school outcasts who randomly kill a woman to enact an amoral philosophy.

almost thirty-four years after his initial incarceration. Just prior to his release, he wrote a memoir, *Life Plus 99 Years*, about his crime, the subsequent hearing, and his life in prison.

Upon his release on parole, Leopold moved to San Juan, Puerto Rico, where he worked for low wages as an X-ray technician at a hospital. He eventually obtained a master's degree and taught at the University of Puerto Rico. He also wrote a book on the birds of Puerto Rico.

Leopold married a former social worker, a widow named Gertrude Feldman Garcia de Quevada, in February 1961. Although their marriage was reportedly unhappy, he remained married to her until his death on August 30, 1971, from natural causes.

Throughout his time in prison, in his memoir, and up to the time of his death, Leopold remembered his deceased friend and criminal accomplice Loeb fondly. However, he also maintained to his dying day that it had been Loeb, not he, who had actually murdered Bobby Franks that infamous day in May 1924.

Notes

Introduction: A Thrill Killing

1. Quoted in *People Weekly*, "Playing For Keeps: Teenage Child-Killers Leopold and Loeb Saw Murder as a Game for Superior Minds," June 14, 1999, p. 141.
2. Hal Higdon, *Leopold and Loeb: Crime of the Century*. Champaign, IL: University of Illinois Press, 1999, p. 97.

Chapter 1: Kidnapping in Kenwood

3. Quoted in Court TV's Crime Library, "Notorious Murders: Leopold & Loeb." www.crimelibrary.com.
4. Quoted in Higdon, *Leopold and Loeb*, p. 40.
5. Quoted in Alvin Sellers, *The Loeb-Leopold Case*. Brunswick, GA: Classic, 1926, pp. 11–12.
6. Quoted in Sellers, *The Loeb-Leopold Case*, pp, 11–12.
7. Quoted in Higdon, *Leopold and Loeb*, p. 42.
8. Quoted in Higdon, *Leopold and Loeb*, p. 45.
9. Quoted in *Chicago Daily News*, "Review of Franks Case Step by Step," September 10, 1924, p. 3.
10. Quoted in Maureen McKernan, *The Amazing Crime and Trial of Leopold and Loeb*, Chicago: Plymouth Court, 1924, p. 11.
11. Quoted in Higdon, *Leopold and Loeb*, p. 47.
12. Quoted in McKernan, *The Amazing Crime and Trial of Leopold and Loeb*, p. 12.

Chapter 2: Manhunt

13. Scott A. Newman, "The Leopold and Loeb Case of 1924," *Jazz Age Chicago*. www.suba.com.
14. Quoted in Court TV's Crime Library, "Notorious Murders: Leopold & Loeb."
15. Quoted in McKernan, *The Amazing Crime and Trial of Leopold and Loeb*, p. 17.
16. Quoted in Higdon, *Leopold and Loeb*, p. 87.
17. Quoted in Higdon, *Leopold and Loeb*, p. 87.

18. Quoted in Higdon, *Leopold and Loeb*, p. 91.

19. Quoted in Higdon, *Leopold and Loeb*, p. 91.

20. Quoted in *Chicago Daily News*, "Review of Franks Case Step By Step," p. 3.

21. Quoted in Court TV's Crime Library, "Notorious Murders: Leopold and Loeb."

22. Quoted in Higdon, *Leopold and Loeb*, p. 93.

23. Quoted in *New York Times*, "State Ending Case of Franks Slayers With Confessions," July 30, 1924, p. 1.

24. Quoted in *New York Times*, "State Ending Case of Franks Slayers With Confessions," p. 1.

25. Quoted in Higdon, *Leopold and Loeb*, p. 112.

26. Quoted in Higdon, *Leopold and Loeb*, p. 126.

27. Quoted in Higdon, *Leopold and Loeb*, p. 112.

Chapter 3: A Perfect Crime

28. Quoted in Marianne Rackliffe, "The Apprehension and Interrogation." Leopoldandloeb.com.

29. Quoted in Court TV's Crime Library, "Notorious Murders: Leopold and Loeb." www.crimelibrary.com.

30 Quoted in Marianne Rackliffe, "The Confessions." Leopold andloeb.com.

31. Quoted in Marianne Rackliffe, "The Confessions." Leopold andloeb.com.

32. Quoted in Douglas O. Linder, "The Confession of Nathan Leopold," Law School, University of Missouri–Kansas City, 1997. www.law.umkc.edu/faculty/projects/ftrials/ leoploeb/Accountoftrial.html.

33. Quoted in McKernan, *The Amazing Crime and Trial of Leopold and Loeb*, p. 26.

34. Quoted in McKernan, *The Amazing Crime and Trial of Leopold and Loeb*, p. 26.

35. Quoted in Nathan F. Leopold, *Life Plus 99 Years*. Garden City, NY: Doubleday, 1957 and 1958, p. 27.

36. Quoted in McKernan, *The Amazing Crime and Trial of Leopold and Loeb*, p. 65.

Chapter 4: An Airtight Case

37. Quoted in Paula S. Fass, *Kidnapped: Child Abduction in America*. New York: Oxford University Press, 1997, p. 58.
38. Quoted in Albert Halper, *The Chicago Crime Book*, Cleveland OH: World, 1967, pp. 273–274.
39. Quoted in McKernan, *The Amazing Crime and Trial of Leopold and Loeb*, p. 68.
40. Quoted in Halper, *The Chicago Crime Book*, p. 275.
41. Quoted in Higdon, *Leopold and Loeb*, p. 145.
42. Quoted in *New York Times*, "Slayers of Franks Both Plead Guilty; Judge Holds Fate," July 22, 1924, p. 1.
43. Quoted in *New York Times*, "Slayers of Franks Both Plead Guilty," p. 1.
44. Quoted in Higdon, *Leopold and Loeb*, p. 173.
45. Quoted in Higdon, *Leopold and Loeb*, p. 176.
46. Quoted in *New York Times*, "Mrs. Franks Heard As Counsel Fights For Son's Slayers," July 24, 1924, p. 1.
47. Quoted in *New York Times*, "Mrs. Franks Heard As Counsel Fights For Son's Slayers," p. 1.
48. Quoted in *New York Times*, "Leopold Would Live, Having 'Work to Do,' Sees No Crime Done," July 26, 1924, p. 1.
49. Quoted in *New York Times*, "Leopold Would Live," p. 1.

Chapter 5: Men of Diseased Minds

50. Quoted in *New York Times*, "State Ending Case of Franks Slayers with Confessions," p. 1.
51. Quoted in McKernan, *The Amazing Crime and Trial of Leopold and Loeb*, p. 80.
52. Quoted in Fass, *Kidnapped*, p. 76.
53. Quoted in Fass, *Kidnapped*, p. 63.
54. Quoted in Sellers, *The Loeb-Leopold Case*, p. 16.
55. Quoted in Sellers, *The Loeb-Leopold Case*, p. 23.
56. Quoted in McKernan, *The Amazing Crime and Trial of Leopold and Loeb*, p. 110.
57. Quoted in McKernan, *The Amazing Crime and Trial of Leopold and Loeb*, p. 111.

58. Quoted in McKernan, *The Amazing Crime and Trial of Leopold and Loeb*, p. 143.
59. Quoted in *New York Times*, "Alienist Declares Leopold and Loeb Are Devoid of Souls," August 5, 1924, p. 1.
60. Quoted in Higdon, *Leopold and Loeb*, p. 218.
61. Quoted in *New York Times*, "State Accuses Girl of Lying for Loeb; Four Chums Testify," August 8, 1924, p. 1.
62. Quoted in Higdon, *Leopold and Loeb*, p. 228.

Chapter 6: Showdown and Decision

63. Douglas O. Linder, "The Leopold and Loeb Trial: A Brief Account," Law School, University of Missouri–Kansas City, 1997. www.law.umkc.edu/faculty/projects/ftrials/leop loeb/Accountoftrial.html.
64. Quoted in Sellers, *The Loeb-Leopold Case*, p. 44.
65. Quoted in Sellers, *The Loeb-Leopold Case*, p. 89.
66. Quoted in Sellers, *The Loeb-Leopold Case*, p. 98.
67. Quoted in Gilbert Geis and Leigh B. Bienen, *Crimes of the Century*, Boston: Northeastern University Press, 1998, p. 18.
68. Quoted in Clarence Darrow, *Attorney for the Damned*, ed. Arthur Weinberg. New York: Simon & Schuster, 1957, p. 20.
69. Quoted in Darrow, *Attorney for the Damned*, p. 21.
70. Quoted in Irving Younger, ed., *Clarence Darrow's Sentencing Speech in* State of Illinois v. Leopold and Loeb. Minnetonka, MN: Professional Education Group, 1993, pp. 2–4.
71. Quoted in Sellers, *The Loeb-Leopold Case*, pp. 132–33.
72. Quoted in Younger, *Clarence Darrow's Sentencing Speech in* State of Illinois v. Leopold and Loeb, p. 19.
73. Quoted in Darrow, *Attorney for the Damned*, p. 77.
74. Quoted in Darrow, *Attorney for the Damned*, pp. 52–53.
75. Quoted in Darrow, *Attorney for the Damned*, p. 82.
76. Quoted in Sellers, *The Loeb-Leopold Case*, p. 242.
77. Quoted in Higdon, *Leopold and Loeb*, p. 242.
78. Quoted in Sellers, *The Loeb-Leopold Case*, pp. 236–37.
79. Quoted in Sellers, *The Loeb-Leopold Case*, p. 305.
80. Quoted in Higdon, *Leopold and Loeb*, p. 247.

81. Quoted in McKernan, *The Amazing Crime and Trial of Leopold and Loeb*, p. 372.
82. Quoted in McKernan, *The Amazing Crime and Trial of Leopold and Loeb*, p. 379–80.

Epilogue: Aftermath

83. Quoted in "Review of Franks Case Step by Step," *Chicago Daily News*, September 10, 1924, p. 1.
84. Quoted in Higdon, *Leopold and Loeb*, p. 267.
85. Quoted in Higdon, *Leopold and Loeb*, p. 269.
86. Quoted in *New York Times*, "The Mercy of the Court," September 11, 1924, p. 22.
87. Leopold, *Life Plus 99 Years*, p. 78.

Timeline

November 19, 1904
Nathan Leopold Jr. is born.

June 11, 1905
Richard Albert Loeb is born.

Fall 1920
Leopold and Loeb meet at the University of Chicago.

February 1921
Leopold and Loeb enter into their secret compact.

1921–1923
Leopold and Loeb commit a series of crimes.

November 1923
Leopold and Loeb begin planning "the perfect crime."

May 21, 1924
Leopold and Loeb kidnap and murder Bobby Franks.

May 22, 1924
Bobby Franks's body is found by Tony Mankowski; Jacob Franks receives the kidnap letter; the body of Bobby Franks is identified.

May 25, 1924
Leopold is brought in for questioning and released.

May 29, 1924
Leopold and Loeb are brought in for questioning.

May 30, 1924
Leopold and Loeb confess to the kidnap and murder. State's Attorney Robert Crowe announces the case is solved and takes Leopold and Loeb on hunt for evidence. Both men are examined by alienists hired by Crowe.

May 31, 1924
Clarence Darrow is hired by the Leopold and Loeb families to represent the accused killers.

June 2, 1924
At a grand jury hearing Leopold and Loeb are indicted on several counts of kidnapping and murder.

June 11, 1924
Leopold and Loeb are arraigned and plead not guilty. Trial date is set for August 4, 1924.

June–July 1924
Leopold and Loeb are examined by alienists for the defense, doctors White, Healy, Glueck, Hulbert, and Bowman.

July 21, 1924
Defendants change plea to guilty with request to present psychological evidence in mitigation of sentence. Motion is accepted and hearing date is moved to July 23, 1924.

July 23, 1924
Hearing begins.

July 30, 1924
Prosecution rests after calling eighty-one witnesses; defense calls first witness, setting off three-day legal duel.

August 12, 1924
Defense rests. Prosecution begins rebuttal of testimony.

August 19, 1924
Prosecution rests again.

August 19–27, 1924
Final arguments are presented by prosecution and defense.

September 10, 1924
Decision by Judge Caverly sentences Leopold and Loeb each to life for murder and ninety-nine years for kidnapping, sentences to run concurrently.

January 28, 1936
Loeb is killed in prison.

March 13, 1958
Leopold is paroled after thirty-four years in prison and moves to Puerto Rico.

February 5, 1961
Leopold marries Gertrude Feldman Garcia de Queveda in Puerto Rico.

August 30, 1971
Leopold dies in Puerto Rico of natural causes.

For Further Reading

Books

Edward W. Knappman, *Great American Trials*. Detroit, MI: Visible Ink Press, 1994. This chronological history of important American trials includes a synopsis of the Leopold and Loeb case.

Meyer Levin, *Compulsion*. New York: Dell, reprint, 1991. Levin's 1956 historical novel depicts a fictionalized version of the Leopold and Loeb case, including a meticulous analysis of the convicted killers.

Michael S. Lief, H. Mitchell Caldwell, and Ben Bycel, *Ladies and Gentlemen of the Jury: Greatest Closing Arguments in Modern Law*. New York: Scribner, 1998. Devoted to the great summations in the history of contemporary law, this book includes a short but summary article highlighting the Leopold and Loeb case with commentary analysis of Clarence Darrow's legal strategy.

Video

History Channel, *In Search of History: Born Killers: Leopold & Loeb*. A&E Television Networks, 1998. This video examines the evidence and contemporary new coverage in the Leopold and Loeb case. Includes interviews with numerous experts in the case and some people who were involved with the case, including Irving Hartman.

Websites

"The Crime of the Century," *People v. Nathan F. Leopold, Jr., and Richard Loeb*, Criminal Court No. 33623 and 33624 (www.cookcountyclerkofcourt.org). A summary of the case from the archives of the Cook County Circuit Court, with links to original legal documents related to the case and useful links to other resources.

Works Consulted

Books

Clarence Darrow, *Attorney for the Damned*. Ed. Arthur Weinberg. New York: Simon & Schuster, 1957. This autobiographical account of Darrow's cases includes an insightful recollection and essay of the Leopold and Loeb case.

Paula S. Fass, *Kidnapped: Child Abduction in America*. New York: Oxford University Press, 1997. This book traces the history of kidnapping in the United States from the 1874 abduction of four-year-old Charley Ross to the 1979 disappearance of Etan Patz. It includes well-researched highlights of the Leopold and Loeb case and others such as the Lindbergh baby and Gloria Vanderbilt kidnappings.

Gilbert Geis and Leigh B. Biemen, *Crimes of the Century*. Boston: Northeastern University Press, 1998. Presents vivid accounts of five of the most famous crimes and trials of the twentieth century. Each case is covered from crime to sentencing with further readings suggested for each case.

Albert Halper, *The Chicago Crime Book*. Cleveland, OH: World, 1967. Historical reference with twenty-five articles portraying significant Chicago crimes and criminals, including an article on Leopold and Loeb.

Hal Higdon, *Leopold & Loeb, The Crime of the Century*. Champaign, IL: University of Illinois Press, 1999. An extremely detailed and well-written account of the Leopold and Loeb case, including biographical material on all major figures. Includes extensive bibliography. No photographs.

Nathan F. Leopold, *Life Plus 99 Years*. Garden City, NY: Doubleday, 1957 and 1958. Written by Leopold during his last years of incarceration, this autobiography details Leopold's life in prison at Joliet and Stateville, including information regarding Richard Loeb's murder.

Maureen McKernan, *The Amazing Crime and Trial of Leopold and Loeb*. Chicago, IL: Plymouth Court, 1924. Written with the assistance of defense attorneys Clarence Darrow and Walter

Bachrach, this book provides detailed information and documentation of the crimes and trial of Leopold and Loeb from the commission of the crime to the sentencing by Judge Caverly.

Alvin V. Sellers, *The Loeb-Leopold Case*. Brunswick, GA: Classic, 1926. A useful and direct historical reporting of documents and testimony related to the crime and hearing.

Irwin Younger, ed., *Clarence Darrow's Sentencing Speech in* State of Illinois v. Leopold and Loeb. Minnetonka, MN: Professional Education Group, 1993. This volume contains the full closing speech delivered by Clarence Darrow in *State of Illinois v. Leopold and Loeb*. Includes a short introduction by Irving Younger.

Periodicals

Chicago Daily News, "Review of Franks Case Step by Step," September 10, 1924.

New York Times, "Alienist Declares Leopold and Loeb Are Devoid of Souls," August 5, 1924.

_____, "Leopold and Loeb Sane, Judge Rules, Jury Trial Denied," August 6, 1924.

_____, "Leopold Would Live, Having 'Work to Do,' Sees No Crime Done," July 26, 1924.

_____, "The Mercy of the Court," September 11, 1924.

_____, "Mrs. Franks Heard as Counsel Fights for Son's Slayers," July 24, 1924.

_____, "Slayers of Franks Both Plead Guilty; Judge Holds Fate," July 22, 1924.

_____, "State Accuses Girl of Lying for Loeb; Four Chums Testify," August 8, 1924.

_____, "State Ending Case of Franks Slayers with Confessions," July 30, 1924.

_____, "Strange Impulses of Franks Slayers Traced to Cradle," August 9, 1924.

People Weekly, "Playing for Keeps: Teenage Child-Killers Leopold and Loeb Saw Murder as a Game for Superior Minds," June 14, 1999.

Internet Sources

Court TV's Crime Library, "Notorious Murders: Leopold and Loeb." www.crimelibrary.com.

Douglas O. Linder, "The Confession of Nathan Leopold," Law School, University of Missouri–Kansas City, 1997. www.law.umkc.edu.

_____, "The Leopold and Loeb Trial: A Brief Account," Law School, University of Missouri–Kansas City, 1997. www.law.umkc.edu.

Scott A. Newman, "The Leopold and Loeb Case of 1924," Jazz Age Chicago. www.suba.com.

Websites

Court TV's Crime Library (www.crimelibrary.com). This site includes articles on numerous crimes and criminals. The section on the Leopold and Loeb case includes synopses of the case, proceedings, and biographical information.

Independence Hall Association (www.ushistory.org). Hosted by the Independence Hall Association, this website includes historical articles and resources for students.

Leopoldandloeb.com (www.leopoldandloeb.com). Marianne Rackliffe's website includes short articles on the Leopold and Loeb case, including biographical information, details about evidence and clues, and synopses of the various stages of the crime and court proceedings.

Index

Picture Credits

Cover photo: © Underwood & Underwood/Corbis
AP/Wide World Photos, 56
© Bettmann/CORBIS, 8, 18, 22, 29, 31, 34, 45, 53, 57, 61, 63, 72,
    75, 78, 82, 87, 91
Hulton/Archive by Getty Images, 25, 26, 49, 68
Chris Jouan, 11, 16, 43
© Underwood & Underwood/CORBIS, 14, 39

About the Author

Andy Koopmans is the author of several books, including biographies of Bruce Lee, Charles Lindbergh, Madonna, and the Osbournes. He is also the author of *Understanding Great Literature: Lord of the Flies* and editor of *Examining Popular Culture: Crimes and Criminals.* He is also a fiction writer, essayist, and poet. He lives in Seattle, Washington, with his wife Angela Mihm and their pets Bubz, Licorice, and Zachary.

He wishes to thank the University of Washington Law Library for their research assistance and his editor Jennifer Skancke for her patience and expertise.

NEW BRIGHTON HIGH SCHOOL
NEW BRIGHTON. PA 15066